Patrick Whiteside trained in medicine at Cambridge University and Guy's Hospital, and in psychiatry in New Zealand and South Australia, and at St George's Hospital Medical School in London. He has been a consultant psychiatrist in the National Health Service since 1988. He likes walking, golfing, reading, travel, photography and film. He is a churchgoing Christian (Anglican), with a mind wide open to the teachings and practices of other Christian denominations and world religions. He is a member of the Buddhist–Christian Network, the Thomas Merton Society, and the Scientific and Medical Network. Find out more at *www.happinesssite.com.*

More praise for Patrick Whiteside:

'Being miserable can become a habit when we forget how to put aside the thoughts that lead us to being miserable and how to find the way of being which makes us happy. Patrick Whiteside shows us how we can recognise our habit of being miserable and how we can have ready access to happiness.' Dorothy Rowe, author of *Depression: The Way Out of Your Prison*

'It is my practice to read something after zazen (meditation) in the morning when my mind is clear and receptive. I have already used *The Little Book of Happiness* for this, and turned eagerly to this new book. I have read it through slowly, twice now, in this fashion, a few pages each day, and I was surprised how hard Patrick made me work. I mean this very much as a compliment. It was a pleasant surprise. I am looking forward to his next book already' James H Austin, author of *Zen and the*

Also by Patrick Whiteside

The Little Book of Happiness
The Little Book of Bliss

HAPPINESS

*The 30-day Guide
that Will Last You a Lifetime*

Patrick Whiteside

RIDER
LONDON · SYDNEY · AUCKLAND · JOHANNESBURG

First published in 2001

5 7 9 10 8 6 4

Copyright © Patrick Whiteside 2001

Published in 2001 by Rider,
an imprint of Ebury Press, Random House,
20 Vauxhall Bridge Road, London SW1V 2SA
www.randomhouse.co.uk

Random House Australia (Pty) Limited
20 Alfred Street, Milsons Point, Sydney,
New South Wales 2061, Australia

Random House New Zealand Limited
18 Poland Road, Glenfield,
Auckland 10, New Zealand

Random House South Africa (Pty) Limited
Endulini, 5A Jubilee Road,
Parktown 2193, South Africa

Random House UK Limited Reg. No. 954009

Papers used by Rider are natural, recyclable products made from wood grown
in sustainable forests.

Printed and bound in Great Britain by CPI Antony Rowe, Eastbourne

A CIP catalogue record for this book
is available from the British Library

ISBN 0-7126-0212-7

*To all my fellow students and
professional colleagues over the years.*

Also in special memory of
Grandad George (1906–78)
My friend Julie (1941–83)
My Godmother Emmy (1915–97)
And for my good friend and teacher Joe (1941–2000),
with love and thanks.

'I believe that the very purpose of our life is to seek happiness.
Whether one believes in religion or not, we are all seeking
something better in life.'

His Holiness The Dalai Lama (b 1935)

'What we are develops in our minds.
All that we are arises with consciousness,
With our thoughts, sense perceptions, impulses and emotions.
With these elements of mind, we make the world.

Speak or act with an impure mind and trouble will follow you,
As the wheel follows the ox pulling the cart.

Speak or act with a pure mind and happiness will follow you
As your shadow, unshakeable.

See the false as false, the true as true.
Look into your heart.
Follow your nature.'

The Sayings of the Buddha (563–483 BC)

'[For me] There is only one unhappiness: not to love God.'
Thomas Merton (1915–68)

Contents

List of Exercises

1 a) How Do I Feel?
   b) How Do I Feel about my Feelings?
   c) Stay with the Feeling.

2 a) Exploring some Difficult Feelings.
   b) Follow your Breath.

3 a) All that Arises Ceases.
   b) How Does it Feel Giving Things Up?

Acknowledgements

The idea to include exercises was originally that of Judith Kendra, the Publishing Director at Rider Books. Thank you Judith. Thanks also to Florence Hamilton for tidying up my text and contributing pertinent insights. Lovely.

Preface

'The very purpose of our life is to seek happiness,' as the Dalai Lama has said. A sense of meaning and purpose in life is an important component of mental health, which is much more than simply the absence of mental illness. Happiness is central to our well-being. Towards it is where we are meant to be going. This is why, as a psychiatrist, I have been investigating it for many years. This has involved exploring happiness – and, in necessary contrast, unhappiness – to the full in my own life, as well as observing it closely in the lives of others.

My exploration continues, and I can say that the benefit to me has already been immense. I am a much happier, more peaceful and contented person than I was. I am eager to share what I have learned, and to offer in this book some practical steps for you to follow.

The nineteenth-century explorer Alexander von Humboldt made the point that if you want to know what a faraway place is really like, it is no good sitting in a library in London, Paris or Rome and reading about it. If you want to know it, not just know about it, you have to make the trip. You have to go there.

Similarly, if you want to know happiness and experience it fully, there are places within your own mind that you need energy, courage, confidence and determination to visit, just as if you were about to embark on a journey. You will also need a serviceable map such as this book can provide, one that demonstrates the underlying logic of human feelings and makes them more manageable. Insightful contemporary ideas and a new theory about a double-sided spectrum of human emotion are seamlessly interwoven with ancient and time-tested wisdom in a fresh, new and easily accessible psychology for our time.

Taken at the right pace, this comprehensive 30-day guide makes things easy without being over-simplified. I suggest you read one chapter per day which will allow and encourage you to reflect on the material. You may feel able to go faster. You may feel comfortable going more slowly, and I advise you to take rest days between chapters. You may find it best to use the Guide only at weekends, when you may have more leisure time and be able to concentrate with a clearer mind. It is up to you to decide.

Happiness includes text and illustrative true stories – in which, to protect the privacy of those concerned, all the names have been changed. It also contains exercises. The text and the exercises complement each other. Both are to be read, and the exercises are there to be done. This, of course, takes a little time, but in most cases you can decide for yourself how long you spend on each. Just a few minutes may be enough.

You may take the exercises as optional. But if you really want to know happiness, not just know about it, you will do them, maybe adapt them, and will want to come back to them, perhaps many times. You are perfectly free to make your own choice about this.

I was raised by my father's oft-repeated dictum, 'You only get out of life what you put into it', coupled with that of St Paul, favoured by my devout and devoted Godmother, 'You reap whatever you sow' (Galatians 6 v 7). In the attempt to map out a pathway to happiness, I have put what I can into writing this book. I have enjoyed doing so, and I hope that you will now reap the benefits too. Put a little something of yourself into it, and I feel sure that you will.

Patrick Whiteside December 2000

Begin at the Beginning

1

Happiness exists in the present moment,
And in the very place where you are. (H 27)[1]

You have to start where you are.

Does one or more of these statements ring true for you?

'I am unhappy and I want to be happy.'

'I am happy, but I want to be happier.'

'I am happy now, and do not want to be unhappy ever again.'

'I know I cannot be happy all the time, but I want to keep unhappiness to a minimum.'

'I am happy but people around me are not, and I would like them to be happy too.'

*

Happiness comes and goes and is a state of mind. It is liable to change as opposed to a personality trait that will last indefinitely. Our characters go on developing throughout our lives, so we can become happier as life progresses. Our experience of happiness can become more intense, more frequent and lasting. This book will show you how to increase your chances of lifelong happiness.

---

[1] Throughout the book quotes at the beginning of each chapter are taken from *The Little Book of Happiness* (H) or *The Little Book of Bliss* (B) followed by the relevant page number.

How Do I Feel?

Sit somewhere quietly for a few minutes and let your thoughts settle, then turn your attention to the question: How do I feel? On balance, at this moment, *am I happy, neutral or unhappy? Then, if you like, say it aloud: 'I feel happy', 'I feel neutral', 'I feel unhappy'.*

Watch what happens to your feelings as you observe them and when you say out loud what they are. Is there any change? Keep observing the condition of your emotions for as long as you feel like it.

Of course, our emotional experience is much broader and richer than simple happiness or unhappiness. As we begin to examine them though, these words can describe feelings that are pleasant on the one hand and unpleasant, even painful, on the other. There will be time to elaborate on this important subject, the spectrum or range of human emotion, later on.

*

The first exercise is a key one in helping us to acquire positive feelings, because it requires skills that we can practise and develop. First there is the simple observation of our emotional state. Then there is giving it a name. Even if you were to put the book away now, having understood this you will have learned something of value.

Emotions carry energy. They are powerful. They colour our thoughts, impulses, speech and actions all the time. Learning to sit quietly and observe them is like activating the clutch when your motor is running. It allows you to feel in control.

Feeling in control is important for most people. Feeling out of control is usually unpleasant. Although it can make us feel good, in the sense of being thrilling or exciting, it more often tends to make us feel anxious. So it is best to find a balance between control and excitement with which both you and the people around you feel comfortable. This is not always easy, and there will be more to say on that subject later.

*

Naming feelings aloud, in a whisper or in the quiet of our inner mental space, as you may have discovered during that first exercise, can result in a change in our feelings. Often we begin to feel okay about them, and so relax and feel better.

This is a subtle but important point. As human beings we not only have emotional sensations, feelings, but we also have feelings about our feelings. For example, if I say, 'I am unhappy and I want to be happy', it means not only that I am unhappy, but also that I am unhappy about being unhappy. I am doubly unhappy! If I then sit quietly and notice that I am unhappy, and then observe out loud to myself, 'Patrick, you are unhappy', it seems to make it easier to come to terms with. I can stop resisting the unpleasant experience and begin to relax about it. I might not become happy about feeling unhappy, but I can at least become neutral about it. The unhappy feeling often goes and soon enough I begin to feel happy again.

On the other hand, if you are happy and note that you are happy, taking the time and making an effort to fully experience that feeling can cause it to expand. This naturally helps the happy feeling to last longer.

How Do I Feel about my Feelings?

Sit quietly again for a few minutes. Focus your mind once more on your emotional state: good, neutral or bad. Say either aloud, in a whisper or to yourself in silence: 'I feel good (or neutral or bad, whichever seems to apply)'. Now, observe again and try to work out how you feel about the first feeling. Repeat what you said before and add: 'And I feel good (or neutral or bad) about that'. If this exercise makes you confused, simply say to yourself: 'I feel confused'. No problem. Give it up, and maybe try again later.

Sometimes there may be a slightly more difficult problem. This is the problem called 'doubt'. If I am sitting feeling bad, and I am unhappy about feeling bad, I may start to think that this bad feeling will never go away. I begin to doubt that it will end.

Similarly, if I am sitting feeling good, and I am happy about feeling good, I may start to think that this good feeling will soon come to an end. I begin to doubt that it will last.

It is good to remember when either of these situations arises that doubt itself is an emotion. Like confusion or bewilderment, it is one of the emotions that go to make up the spectrum of unhappiness. It too gives rise to negative thoughts. We will consider the relationship between thoughts and emotions more carefully later on. For now you can take comfort in the idea that emotional experiences do not persist without impetus, without being reinforced somehow. Unless there is something to fuel them and keep them going, the natural thing is for them to alter in quality and soften in intensity with time. We will be looking at how this works throughout the book.

Stay with the Feeling.

Sit quietly again, and be prepared to sit a little longer this time. Wait until your thoughts settle then ask yourself again, 'How am I feeling right now? Am I feeling good, neutral or bad?' Stay with that feeling for a time. Observe it.

Try to be patient. After a while ask yourself, 'Is this feeling going to last? About how long?' Now continue to observe what happens to your thoughts and feelings. Give up the exercise whenever you choose, but also think about trying it again at another time. See if you can identify when certainty changes to doubt, and whether doubt brings with it the impulse to quit. ·

Doubt, when it arises, usually comes with the thought that what you are doing is not worthwhile. The impulse to stop whatever you are doing when doubt arises can be very strong. The same impulse often attends other unpleasant emotional experiences such as confusion, and feelings of anxiety or anger. It can be interesting and useful to try and be patient with the unpleasant feelings, to observe them and wait for them to subside. This is not always easy to do, but again it is a skill that each one of us can practise and develop. It is an excellent way of learning how to become more emotionally mature.

What is Suffering?

2

Sit quietly for a while
Undistracted
Every day. (H 39)

The word 'suffering' is usually synonymous with pain, physical or emotional pain, or with deprivation. There are however three possible meanings, of which this is only one. It is instructive to look at the others.

'To suffer' can mean simply to experience. This permits the use of the word in regard to neutral and pleasant things as well as those that are unpleasant. 'I suffered delight on receiving the invitation', is equally valid as a statement in English as is, 'I suffered anxiety at being kept waiting'. The point here is that people are probably conditioned to take note of unhappy experiences more than of happy ones. Happily, this conditioning can be changed. And a clue as to how it can be changed can be found in the third possible meaning of the verb 'to suffer'.

The third meaning of 'to suffer' is to permit or allow. The best-known example comes from the New Testament of the Bible when Jesus is reported as saying, 'Suffer the little children to come unto me, and forbid them not'.[2] As well as to permit, it can even be extended to mean to encourage. This is useful when thinking about

[2] St Mark 10 v 14.

emotions, even painful emotions. And this is because resisting painful emotions usually results in strengthening them and making them last.

In simple terms, we resist our emotions whenever we feel bad about them. If we are unhappy about feeling unhappy, then we are stuck with that feeling. Once we accept it, grow neutral about it, we can and naturally do begin to let go of it.

For example, sometimes when I begin to feel angry with someone close to me, perhaps someone I love and respect, I begin to feel ashamed or guilty about my own anger. This is one type of bad feeling about another type. The shame and guilt distract me from the anger briefly, but somehow I know it is still there. Because it is unpleasant to feel ashamed or guilty, I will often start to feel angry again, and focusing on my anger fuels the shame and guilt once more. A vicious cycle begins, and there are many similar scenarios in the realm of human emotion. But there is a way out.

If you feel angry, either with a loved one or an enemy, whether justified or not, it is you who experiences the painful emotion, no-one else. If you also feel shame or guilt at your own anger, you are in a trap from which the escape may appear paradoxical; it is really to *suffer* – in the sense of to permit, to experience, even to encourage the painful emotion, rather than to resist it. This means coming to feel okay about anger, feeling okay about shame and guilt too. Why not? These are essential and inescapable experiences for everyone who is alive.

2

Exploring some Difficult Feelings.

Sit quietly for a few moments. Let your thoughts settle. Now bring to mind an occasion when something or someone made you feel angry. Pay attention to any other feelings that arise. Can you name them? What thoughts are associated with these feelings? Are they worthy, neutral or unworthy thoughts? How much energy are you experiencing? How strong are your feelings?

Now, think of another example. Bring to mind an occasion when something or someone made you feel anxious or fearful. Go through the same questions. Do this again later with guilt, with sadness, and then with joy and satisfaction.

Compare all these emotions. Observe your thoughts and feelings for a few more minutes. How easy or difficult is it for you to let go of the anger and the other feelings? Is it easier if you make a conscious effort to allow the feelings into your mind, to facilitate or encourage them?

Do not worry if you are finding this exercise too time-consuming or difficult. Persevere just as long as you want. You can return to it later whenever you wish.

This exercise and those in the first chapter are not easy to do. There are several reasons for this, the most common of which can be called 'conditioning'.

Few people have been educated or conditioned to examine their emotional lives in such detail. Even to be able to sit quietly by oneself in an undistracted way for anything more than just a few moments is a comparatively uncommon skill, but it is also one of uncommon value. Before continuing to examine emotions, happy and unhappy, it may be better to look a little more closely at 'just sitting'.

*

Sitting comfortably and still on a chair or a cushion with an upright posture for ten, twenty minutes or longer in a quiet, darkened place, with one's eyes shut or almost, allows a special and rewarding close observation of one's own mind, of the content of consciousness, particularly if the process is repeated daily or twice daily for many months. If you have never tried to do this, it may be difficult and off-putting at first. We are so conditioned against wasting time, and sitting doing nothing does often seem like just a waste of time; but it is not.

The practice of calmly observing the content of one's mind is called 'meditation'. This may alarm you. You may be thinking that you will somehow lose control of your own mind, or that someone else may take it over, but in fact the opposite is true. Sitting quietly as described, without distraction, cannot be harmful – for it is simply this: being with yourself.

It is true that simply being with yourself, if you are not used to it, can feel strange and even unpleasant at first, but this is just the point. Become familiar with what at first seems unpleasant and it will eventually no longer feel that way. It will fairly soon seem to feel neutral (and possibly still a waste of time). Later on it will come to feel good. With practice and experience, being with yourself becomes something more.

Some people[3] refer to the process, which is a discipline, as *'Bringing the mind home'*. It is a comforting idea. We arrive at where we belong.

Being with yourself like this is an exercise in both holding firm and letting go: holding firm to a still posture and to the present moment as it unfolds, letting go of distractive thoughts, impulses and sense perceptions arising with your emotions. It is a reliable method for improving general well-being. Some of the benefits of regular practice can include increased energy, improved concentration, enhanced creativity, greater self-esteem and a longer life.

At each sitting, action is reduced, stilled almost completely except for the inward and outward flow of the breath. Because the intention is to remain seated and still, the impulse to act also soon begins to diminish. Without movement and with the eyes closed, especially in a darkened and quiet room, input to the mind from the senses is equally reduced. This leaves mainly thoughts and emotions to occupy consciousness.

Thoughts and emotions are the most persistent experiences, but they too subside in time and become clearer. This happens more quickly, of course, the more experienced a person becomes at this kind of sitting practice. Importantly too, thoughts and emotions separate out from each other, and come to seem not only less complicated but also more accessible. To put it another way, just as a glass of fruit juice becomes increasingly transparent as time passes and the dregs settle, so during silent sitting the mind becomes increasingly clear. And clarity, of course, is the reverse of confusion. Clarity of mind, we can say with some confidence, almost always feels good.

---

[3] Notably the contemporary Buddhist monk and teacher, Sogyal Rinpoche, in his book, *The Tibetan Book of Living and Dying*.

Follow Your Breath.

Find or prepare a quiet place for yourself where for up to ten or twenty minutes you will not be disturbed. Draw the curtains or darken the room, but not completely. If you wish, light a candle. Choose a quiet time, with no loud noises nearby if possible.

Now, sit quietly, as upright as possible without discomfort, hands resting in a relaxed way in your lap or on the tops of your legs. Close your eyes, either completely or only nearly so (leaving them open just a little will help you avoid falling asleep).

Pay attention at first to the sensation of your weight on the chair or cushion, perhaps of your feet on the floor. Note your breathing. Do not be concerned whether it is fast or slow, shallow or deep. Just note what is happening without trying to control it. Follow the breath in and out a few times (to make use of one of the rhythms in your life which is already present). Stay conscious of your breathing throughout the sitting period if you wish.

Stay alert, but relax too as well as you can. Stop when you feel ready, after one minute if that is all you can manage, after five, ten or twenty minutes. Especially at the beginning, it is best not to go on after half an hour (even if you are feeling very comfortable and mellow). However short or long your sitting, you can always come back to it and practise it again another time, ideally at least once a day.

By now it will be becoming clearer that even painful emotions are worthwhile, because they form part of the path to more secure and lasting happiness. If you follow the guidance in this book, you will eventually become convinced of the wisdom of this.

The Paradox of Misery

3

Getting what you want makes you happy
Knowing what you want can be hard.
What you really want is happiness itself. (H 10)

What do you like? Who do you like? What do you love? Who do you love? If you were surrounded all the time by what you like and by people you love, logic says you would be happy. Why is this not always true?

It is not always true because of our imagination, and because things change. We can imagine things changing for the better, and we can imagine things changing for the worse. This is natural. Things do change for better or worse in nature.

Satiety, or excess, is one problem. This means you have had enough of something, even of something (or someone) you really like. How many ice creams or chocolates can you eat?

Anxiety is another problem. This is the fear that what you have will evaporate or be taken away. Anxiety is the natural reaction to threat.

Satiety can be overcome by patience and restraint. If you wait long enough, you will in time be hungry again for what you like. Often, though, we do not wait. We seek new pleasures, new distractions, or turn again to other favourites. This can become a never-ending pursuit. To obtain true and enduring satisfaction like this is rare.

3

Anxiety is more difficult to overcome. It requires patience, and it also requires wisdom. This is because deep inside we each carry the knowledge that nothing, no-thing and no relationship, will last forever, however much we try to hold on and make it last. In the final analysis this is because we ourselves are finite. We ourselves must one day face death. This is a real threat to our happiness!

All that Arises Ceases.

Sit quietly or, if you would rather, go outside for a short walk. Whether walking or sitting, look around you. Notice a few things that you like and appreciate. Think about how they came into being. If they are yours, think of how you acquired them. Now spend a few moments thinking about what might happen to these precious things as time goes by. Can you think of anything that you will not one day have to give up?

Notice the emotions, the feelings that such thoughts give rise to as you sit still or walk along. You may want to talk to somebody close about this later on.

This can be a powerful exercise and, for some, an upsetting one. The real answer to anxiety is to grieve, to suffer the pain of grief and then allow your grief to resolve. Strangely then, the path to true happiness lies through letting go as opposed to holding on, and through the painful feelings of grief, through suffering these emotions in the sense of experiencing and of allowing them. The wise encourage their misery and grief.

This is a paradox, is it not? Here is a guide to happiness that encourages suffering. Surely, you will think, there must be some other way. I wish there were.

A man and a woman meet. They fall in love. They try to see each other all the time, and when they are apart to keep in contact. How do they know that they care for each other? By how much it hurts to be separated.

To want something or someone, to desire, is already to suffer painful emotions. There is anxiety when the object of your desire is present. And there is grief when it goes or is lost. Lock up your treasure (or your beloved) in a tower, make your home a fortress or prison, and something essential is lost. Even if you deny it, your delight will already be ruined. It is worth thinking about this. Later on, in Chapters 28 and 29, we will explore a more positive view about this.

How Does it Feel Giving Things Up?

Sit quietly again.

It is easier to think about difficult or painful matters if one is calm, silent and alone. Wisdom is often found within ourselves in this simple way. Later we can talk to others about our thoughts, feelings and discoveries.

Sit still quietly for a few minutes, recollecting yourself. Avoid distractions. When you feel comfortable, bring to mind again something (an activity, an object, a pet or a person) that brings you great comfort and pleasure. Experience the satisfaction and joy. Spend a little time on this.

Now think of something that is no longer available to you that once gave you similar pleasure, something you have had to give up. Allow yourself to experience the new feelings. How are they different? Can you feel the same level of satisfaction and joy? Is there also some tinge of distress, of sorrow? Is there still some reluctance to let the past go, some irritation or anger? What other feelings arise? If you can, whisper or say the names of these emotions out loud.

Relax again. Bring your mind back to the present, to the here and now. Open your eyes fully. Look around. You have survived the loss. You are safe. Sit breathing quietly again for a moment until you feel like getting up. Go on. Continue your day.

If you have entered fully into this exercise, there may be some after-shocks. It is best to have a confidant, someone to talk to, someone you trust with your deepest thoughts and feelings.

It is important to have confidence in the processes of emotional pain, of grief and healing. In this book we are going to identify the painful emotions and contrast them with those that are pain-free. We will be showing how the first group, the unpleasant ones, naturally and spontaneously give rise to those that are pleasant, unless we hinder the process ourselves.

With confidence and courage we can develop the natural and healthy responses to loss and threat. Gradually, loss can be faced with greater equanimity. The tensions of anxiety slowly relax, giving way to calmer feelings of peace. Greater levels of joy and happiness will surely accompany both.

The Well of Happiness 4

There is really nothing for you to learn
That your mind does not already know.
It knows how to be happy.
Like you, it wants to be happy and calm. (H 52)

Initially, ideas like these can be hard to understand and accept. They can be seen as 'counter-intuitive'. Unfortunately quite a lot of wisdom turns out to be like this, but this is what makes the distinction between wisdom and common sense.

In our search for happiness, wisdom seeks to penetrate deeper into the nature of human reality. How can our minds know things that we ourselves do not? It seems like an insoluble mystery, but it can be made accessible. Indeed, through a deep and natural form of intuition, some people know this already. This is different from everyday intuition, which has been at least partially conditioned or affected by learning and worldly experience.

*

There is an ancient proverb about how to draw water successfully from a well.[4] It is important to have a rope that is long enough and to let it down all the way. It is also important that your bucket is strong, capacious and not full of holes.

---

[4] From hexagram 38 of 'The Book of Changes' (otherwise known as *I Ching*).

4

To be able to draw forth happiness, peace and wisdom from within ourselves like our bucket, we need to be whole. We need to be properly prepared, careful, capable of both concentration and perseverance. Our greatest asset in the search for happiness is our own mind. *'The key to the treasure is the treasure'* (H 123). We must learn to use the mind itself in order to obtain the blessings hidden within it.

Imagine Approaching a Well

Sit quietly for a few minutes. Adopt a good posture, with a straight back and slightly raised head. Let your hands fall comfortably in your lap. Let your eyes, almost closed, be directed downward just in front of you without lowering your head.

Let your thoughts and feelings settle. Now, begin to imagine yourself approaching a fairly deep well on a hot summer's day. Use all your senses. Feel the warmth on your skin. Listen to the wind in the dry branches of a nearby tree, and in the background the mechanical sounds of the cicadas. You are thirsty. You have just picked up a bucket. In your mind's eye, examine it closely. Is it new or old? Is it too small or too large for the purpose? Will you need to keep going back to the well or, when it is full, will it be too heavy to lift? Is it rusted, or are there any holes in it that will need to be fixed before you can use it?

Now, using your imagination, turn your attention to a rope neatly coiled beside you. Reach for it and examine it carefully. Gauge its length and its strength. If you think it will do, tie it securely to the handle of your bucket. Now approach the well, let the bucket down with the rope until it reaches the cool, clear water waiting for collection. Notice any obstacles, and whether your rope reaches easily enough to the bottom of the well. Wait until you are sure that the bucket is filled, and now draw it carefully back to the surface. Untie the rope and coil it neatly, so that you and others may use it again, before helping yourself to a well-earned, thirst-quenching drink. When you have had enough and are no longer thirsty, stand still and survey the landscape around you. Listen. Now put the bucket carefully down.

Now you can relax. Stretch and open your eyes.

This exercise is more than just a game. Do not worry if you found it too difficult, or perhaps too boring, to finish. Think about this. Few people in a modern industrialised country ever have to draw water from a well, but many people throughout the world do so daily. At one level then the exercise is instructive about the lives of others. It also reminds us to be present in the here and now as we go about our business, and to be aware with all our senses of what is going on in our environment from moment to moment. The exercise is helpful too in drawing our attention to how much preparation and care we could be using whenever engaged in all our daily tasks, and how considerate of others we could also be if we chose.

How much thought do we each give to where the water from our taps and showers comes from, to the work others have done and are doing for us in bringing water to our homes? Only perhaps when things go wrong, and when we are forced to call in a plumber. It helps to remember, and in the mind's eye to savour, the effort of going to a well with a simple rope and a bucket. It helps us keep the everyday things in our lives in perspective, and this will help us stay happy.

This exercise can also be useful as a metaphor. The water of wisdom, of happiness and of peaceful tranquillity is there in the depths of our beings for each of us to approach and draw from whenever we need to. It is there even if we are not aware of it, even for those among us who have never yet obtained and made use of a suitable bucket and a long enough rope. The first step of course is to realise that you are thirsty.

What are the Sources of Wisdom, Joy and Peace in your Life?

Sit quietly or go for a short walk, perhaps in a park, by a lake or river, or in some other open space where you will not be overly distracted. Spend a few minutes thinking about your life, about where you go for emotional and spiritual sustenance. What are the sources of wisdom, joy and peace in your life? How do you access them? How thirsty are you for these blessings? How successful are you at obtaining them? Did it ever occur to you that the biggest reservoir of your own happiness already lies within yourself?

Stay with this idea a little longer. What emotions does it generate within you: feelings of hope, of confidence, or feelings of doubt? Notice how doubt can make you want to turn away from the idea, to deny it, to say it cannot be true. Ask yourself, 'How do I really know what is true?' Try carrying this question around with you for a day or two, returning to consider it from time to time. You might like to try it out too on your friends.

Truth and wisdom are linked closely. To get at wisdom is also to get at truth. But this is a special kind of truth. It is truth from every angle at once. Because this kind of total truth is hard to achieve in any given situation, an honest person will often be in the position of having to admit, 'I do not know'. Recognising that you do not, and cannot, know everything is the beginning of wisdom, and is often too the beginning of the search for wisdom. The moment you recognise that you are thirsty is the moment you begin seeking something to drink.

Truth, wisdom, peace and happiness: somehow these are all connected, and the most essential place where this link-up occurs is within our minds. If you bring the bucket of a receptive, open mind, books like this can provide the rope, can show you how to discover the wherewithal to get at that water and quench your thirst for joy, to make it happen, to make it happen time and again, to make it happen at will.

Our Marvellous Minds 5

Here is another suggestion that seems to run counter to common sense. You can discover how to feel good by aiming at being more neutral.

The obvious approach would be to discover what makes you feel happy and work hard to get and keep those things. But the problem is that anxiety and satiety get in the way. We fear losing what we have, or we become bored with it and start looking for something else.

What we want is happiness itself. What we do not know, what we seem to have forgotten, is that we have an everlasting source of it to tap into inside ourselves already. This, for the moment, for those who doubt it, needs to be taken on trust.

One argument in favour of the idea is that whenever happiness is triggered by something good, the pleasant taste of ice-cream for example, it is the ice-cream which triggers the taste and the taste which triggers the happy feeling. The origin of this happiness is not in the ice-cream but must already lie somewhere within the mind of the person with taste-buds on their tongue.

It is also true that you can be happy for no particular reason. There does not have to be any identifiable cause triggering feelings of happiness, so again the capacity for feeling good must lie within us. Furthermore, there are occasions when someone with good cause to feel unhappy, because they are in physical pain, for example, feels happy instead. The pain is felt, but the person's equanimity remains intact. There is another important lesson in this.

Equanimity implies a positive balance between painful and pleasant emotions. It also implies resilience, the rapid and sure return of a person's emotional state towards equilibrium after any strong emotional experience (whether painful or pleasant). The thing for you to note is that equanimity is itself free of pain, a happy state, even though the word makes it sound neutral.

This is a subtle point, which explains how we can discover how to feel good by aiming at feeling neutral. The essential paradox here is that feeling neutral feels good!

Now, consider this, it is possible to feel too good. For one thing, it is hard to sustain.

Imagine Feeling Good.

Sit quietly for a few minutes. Let your thoughts and your feelings settle. After a while, bring to mind something simple which gives you pleasure: freshly cut flowers, perhaps, or the smell of new-mown grass, chocolate or a cup of tea, the warmth of sunshine, the sight of new-born lambs. Reflect on how it is that something outside you stirs up something within, feelings of joy, pleasure and satisfaction.

Now take it a step further. Reflect on the feeling of pleasure conjured up by something outside yourself. Pay attention to it and, while it lasts, see what else might be linked with it in your mind. Now try for an instant to experience this pleasure as unattached to whatever first triggered it for you. Try and experience pure pleasure, with no particular focus or cause.

In time ask yourself, 'How do I feel, at this moment?' If the answer is, 'I feel happy', a little later ask yourself, 'Why? How come? How did it come about that I was feeling happy?' Check out whether you do not really know why. You just felt happy because you felt happy – because for a moment or two you had reached the source of happiness. Do not worry if this is not the case, if this was not your experience. Take it on trust for now that you can experience genuine happiness whatever your life circumstances, because it is already there.

Some would say that this capacity for happiness is simply part of human psychology, a result of many thousands of years of evolution. Others would call it a gift by the grace of God. These views are not necessarily in opposition, but the important thing is to hold an open mind. Don't close it prematurely with a belief about 'ultimate cause' before exploring the way things really are. We will return to these difficult matters towards the end of the book.

If happiness truly lies ready to awaken within us, what prevents each one of us having access to it all the time? This is an important question, and there are many ways to look at it. First we are going to examine the more problematic and painful emotions, to see how they tend to arise and how best to restore equanimity when they do. But it is not to be simply an intellectual examination. With the help of exercises, it will be an experiential one. To make progress towards happiness, we will each need to explore the hindrances we meet in everyday life. As with drawing water from a well, it is possible to be successful and to avoid mishap if one takes certain precautions. So we are wise to begin by focusing on the likelihood of our personal equanimity holding sway as we enter the shadows of the less pleasant emotions.

Sitting Still and in Silence.

Sit still for one, five, ten or twenty minutes, whatever you think you can manage.

Try to sit. Nothing else. Simply sit.

Sit silently. Sit in a quiet, somewhat darkened place, comfortably and with a good posture as before. Sit and let your mind go. Set your mind free and also attend very lightly to its content. Listen, feel and watch as distractions arise: sounds, sensations, impulses, images and ideas. Observe and experience these, but try not to hold on to or follow them. Wait, and watch how as time passes they settle.

When the allotted time has passed, simply open your eyes. Stretch a little. Continue your life.

The purpose of this exercise is to experience consciousness, to begin to experience it as something distinct from the content of consciousness. Consciousness is impersonal, but we experience the content of consciousness as if it is somehow our own. Do not worry if you do not follow this yet.

Human minds are of course remarkable in their capabilities. Happiness is an emotion, but alongside emotion there are three other major basic mental processes going on at the same time. There is input from the senses, and output in the form of impulses that generate action. Between input and output, there is also thinking. These four categories (or dimensions) of simultaneous mental activity are integrated and interwoven seamlessly within the healthy mind, but cannot all be held distinct from each other within consciousness at any one moment. The Quadrant diagram below may help you visualise how this interaction might work.

Quadrant Diagram

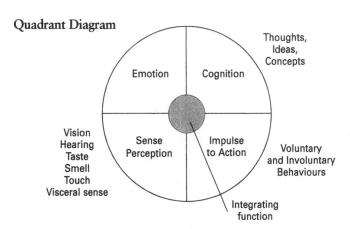

If we think of a stage upon which a scene has been set, we can see how consciousness may impact upon it as if it were a floodlight, illuminating much but highlighting nothing. This is useful, but even so there may be dark places, places further away or in shadow, which cannot be seen. Similarly, consciousness may act as a spotlight, focused and highly concentrated, capable of moving over the scene or landscape so that whatever it hits stands out clearly. This is good, but of course whatever is not spotlit by consciousness will seem more in the dark, less distinct, and so easier to ignore.

Sitting still and observing the changing content of our minds allows us to appreciate how consciousness works and make better use of it. It helps us too to realise that at no time can we be aware of everything going on in our minds, even in 'floodlight' mode. Fortunately, it also helps us to realise that we have no need to. We are utterly free to trust in the continuous and seamless process of integration of sensation, thinking, emotion and action within our marvellous minds, as we trust in the beating of our hearts.

Staying in Focus 6

Take a breath . . . Keep breathing.
Sit still and close your eyes.
Sitting still, listen carefully.
Listen to your breath in the silence. (H 82)

Happiness is an emotion, or perhaps a group of emotions. It is not in itself a sensory experience, a thought or an impulse. There may be the sensation of a warm inner glow when we are happy. Our thoughts may be influenced positively by the emotion. Our impulses and actions may similarly be affected; but there is definitely a distinction between emotion and these other categories of mental activity, so it is on the emotions that we are to focus in this quest for greater, more frequent and more lasting happiness in our lives.

First, in order to maintain this focus, we must learn to take care of distracting sensations, thoughts and impulses. Also, it will be helpful for us to be able to distinguish thoughts about emotion from the experience of emotions themselves.

We are often held back from the experience of emotion by the strength of our reason and our intellect, and we need to be aware of that. We should similarly note that strong emotions also influence our thinking, often in a way that detracts from rationality, from unbiased logic, from pure reason. These are important but potentially confusing considerations, for you simply to note at the moment. We will look into them more closely later, when we explore the emotions associated with cognitive confusion, principally those of doubt and bewilderment.

Focus your Mind on the Senses – and on Awareness Itself.

Take off your shoes. Sit quietly for a few moments until you feel settled and comfortable. Move your right foot so that only the tip of your great toe is touching the floor. Now, for a few seconds, pay attention only to the sensation of that toe. Feel the location of it within your body, and the pressure on the toe from the floor. Experience the texture of the floor's surface. Note the quality of the information available to you when the spotlight of consciousness is sharply focused like this. Notice how little else you are aware of when your mind holds only onto your great toe as it rests on the floor.

Now relax again. Open your eyes without looking at anything in particular, but keeping your head still. Try to take in as much as you can of the room or the view wherever you are. How broad a vista can you be aware of at one time? How aware are you of things attracting your notice, seeming to want you to bring your mind to bear more directly upon them? Things that move usually do this, also things that shine or are brightly lit. Words, writing, signs often seem to stand out as well, tempting us to read them and find out what they mean.

Now try this again with your hearing. What stands out when you listen? Try focusing on the softer sounds. You may find it easier to concentrate if you close your eyes once again.

Now, relax again with your eyes almost (or completely) closed and use your mind's eye to look within. Focus on the content of consciousness. Try to keep your mind open to the broad vista of sensations, thoughts, emotions and impulses that arise. Again, do you notice some that seem to attract your attention, to want to hold the focus of your mind upon them? Try for a little longer to just let everything go.

When you are ready, open your eyes.

At the beginning when sitting down for an exercise like this, many distractions in the form of sensations, thoughts, emotions and impulses will arise. That is why a number of techniques have been devised to help us overcome such distractions. The secret of all these techniques is to provide a repetitive and low energy focus for the mind to use as an anchor. This is not particularly mysterious. The anchor can be a simple word or phrase. It can be a visual image, or it can be the rhythmic inhalation and exhalation of one's own breath. There are countless methods, as many have discovered serendipitously for themselves.

It is not really surprising that some method, some discipline, is required for this activity. After all, sense perceptions: vision, hearing, touch, taste and smell, provide a whole universe of the mind to be explored. Impulses, plus the actions and reactions of muscles together form another such universe. Thinking, symbols, numbers, words, concepts, ideas, memory and imagination provide a third, the universe of 'cognition'.

If we are to explore only (or mainly) emotions, the fourth such kingdom of human experience, we are going to require good concentration and focus. We are going to need the skill of holding our minds alert and steady, with consciousness fixed in the present moment, on the here and now.

Sitting and Walking.

Sitting or walking: first make your choice.

It is sometimes easier to maintain your mind alert and in focus if you are upright and active. Distractions or sleepiness become too much to cope with if you are drowsy, or if you find yourself easily disturbed while sitting on a cushion or in a chair.

If your choice is sitting, *simply sit still and in silence for twenty minutes. If your mind strays, that is all right. Do not struggle with it. Pick a focus. The breath is a good one. Watch the breath. Watch the in-breath, then the out-breath. Count each breath if necessary to keep the mind in focus. Count up to four and start again. If your mind strays, with a little practice you will find it drifts naturally of its own accord back to the breath. If it does not return in this way, you can give it gentle assistance. When you notice your mind straying from your focus, just gently bring it right back. As many times as this happens, do not worry. Simply draw your mind gently back to the breath.*

Decide whether you will listen to the sound of the breath, or pay attention rather to the sensation of air passing first one way, then the other through the nostrils or your partly open mouth. Alternatively, focus on the rise and fall of the chest and abdomen with each breath. Try each one and discover which suits you best. Pay no great attention to whether the breaths are deep or shallow, rapid or slow, but simply note these characteristics of each breath. If you start thinking about your breathing or anything else during

6

this exercise that distracts you, just relax and start again. Keep your mind gently in focus until a kind of still-point is reached.

If your choice is walking, make sure you have space. You can walk up and down in a straight line, perhaps twelve paces in each direction, or you can walk clockwise in a circle. You can do this inside or outside, as you prefer, if there is room.

Remember, this is walking for the sake of walking. It is not walking to get anywhere. Before you begin, stand upright with your arms relaxed beside you or held loosely together in front. Hold your head up and your back straight, but direct your eyes half-closed towards the ground just a few feet in front of you.

When you set off, do so at a slow and regular pace. Maintain this throughout the exercise. If you are walking in a line, turn around at the same spot each time and make your return. Focus your mind on the soles of your feet. (If it is convenient, you may prefer to do this exercise barefoot.) Pay attention as you lift each foot in turn, move it forward rhythmically and replace it on the ground. Notice how different parts of the foot are in contact with the surface in a regular sequence, first one foot and then the other. Continue, and if your mind drifts off, first take notice, stop walking and then, as you set off again, bring your awareness gently back to the movements of your ankles and feet.

Whether sitting or walking, simply continue until twenty minutes have passed. When the allotted time is up, stop and congratulate yourself. You have accomplished something that will prove very useful.

There is an ancient saying: '*Everyone knows the usefulness of the useful, but no one knows the usefulness of the useless*'.[5]

It may not seem useful to be able to sit quietly and still for twenty minutes, or to walk slowly in a circle for the same length of time, but it is. It is useful in terms of observing the mind, and in learning how to combat intrusive, sometimes painful disturbances. The key element involves being able at will to hold the mind in the present, in the here and now.

[5] From *Inner Chapters* by Chuang Tsu, written in China probably in the 4th century BC.

A Good Bucket and a
Long-enough Rope

Stay in the moment!
Happiness can only exist in the present,
In the here and now of your life. (H 26)

The common sense view of happiness is that it depends on something happening, upon our getting and holding onto something that gives pleasure. The alternative view is that happiness is something the capacity for which we each already have within ourselves. Our problem is, we often seem to have forgotten where to find it and how to reach it.

The first view is not only mistaken, but also gets in the way of finding real happiness. This point will become clearer if we examine the relationship between happiness and time. We will also take a look at how memory and imagination work, both of which can increase the risk of our becoming unhappy. This will help us begin to appreciate the usefulness of keeping our minds focused in the present.

Our marvellous minds are something like television sets, each with thousands of channels. Focusing on the present is like switching on and simply watching what is there before you, avoiding indiscriminate channel-hopping. However, in everyday life we change channels frequently, and to do so we sometimes use both memory and imagination. These faculties operate quite naturally, almost all the time we are awake. Certain basic needs have to be fulfilled. On waking, we have to wash, use the toilet, clothe ourselves, find something to eat and drink. Right away we have to visualise things, recall where they are and remember how to engage with them successfully. But we do not always remember to enjoy the most basic activities with which we start every day.

Your Morning Routine.

Sit quietly for a few moments. When comfortably settled, replay your morning routine in your mind's eye. How much attention do you normally pay to each part of it? How much attention do you pay, for example, to the feel of the carpet under your feet as you get out of bed and take a few steps? Or is your mind already full of other things, of things you have to get done?

Reflect sincerely on this for a few moments.

Now ask yourself about your priorities during those first waking minutes. Do you ever pay close attention to what you are actually doing? If so, are you not more likely to be feeling satisfied, happy and calm? If not, are you not more likely to be feeling dissatisfied, anxious and rushed?

Answer these questions for yourself. Answer them honestly. Reflect on them for a few moments more, and then let them go from your mind. Focus again for several moments on the present, on the here and now, on your breath, inward and outward. Are you beginning to feel any calmer?

Getting in touch with the well or source of happiness within is more satisfactory than searching our minds for a happy memory. Getting in touch with that source is also a good first step in encouraging happy thoughts, images and memories.

Recalling moments of pleasure and satisfaction can lead to feelings of happiness, but we usually do this as an escape from unhappiness in the present. The memory of happiness is bound to be less authentic, and less successful in the sense of being shorter-lasting and less satisfying, than happiness genuinely experienced in the present. If it is an escape, it can only be a temporary one, and the gloom we feel may seem all the darker and more miserable if our present predicament is compared with a more pleasurable one from the past. But to be able to find genuine happiness with the help of our innate sense of equanimity, even in disadvantageous circumstances, is very useful.

When things seem to be going badly, we tend to use imagination, instead of or as well as memory, to feel better. But if you are thirsty, standing by a well with a rope that is too short and a bucket full of holes, thinking about the bucket when it was new and visualising a much longer rope is not going to help. Sometimes, this is how it is in life.

We are good at fooling ourselves very often, are we not? We can make believe that things are less serious than they really are. We ignore real threats and real (if gradual) losses, at least until they begin to bite. This is natural. And it is necessary for everyday psychological survival, because the truth is that everything to which we are attached must eventually be given up. Everything we hold dear is ultimately threatened.

This is because to be mortal is to be finite. But dwelling on this can bring us unnecessary pain and suffering too. So we use our imagination, and the memory of painful earlier losses, against ourselves. How easy it is to imagine disaster, is it not? What might the remedy be?

*

Let us use the well of happiness as a metaphor again. To draw forth the water of joy, we need a long enough rope and a good, whole bucket. A bucket full of holes simply sprays water everywhere, just like a mind that squanders or dissipates the potential treasures it contains, and is reluctant to focus or concentrate. The rope represents our need to be diligent and persevering, to make the necessary effort and to apply it for long enough. These ideas are obviously closely related, and a concept that unites them successfully (so that the rope is long and strong enough and the bucket capacious and whole) is 'discipline'. Discipline, then, is part of the remedy. The trick is for you to see this discipline as joyful, not as an unwelcome obligation or chore.

Another part of the remedy is honesty, ruthless and uncompromising truthfulness at all times. Another is simply to dwell forever in the present moment, in the here and now. Be aware of the past. Be aware of the future, take appropriate precautions and make appropriate plans but, having done so, be adaptable and live life firmly anchored in the present, in the very time and very place where you are.

Yesterday has gone. We have access to it using our memories, but how much can we remember? Not everything. How much can we truly remember, without distortion? Even less. And how much of today will we miss by spending time remembering yesterday?

Similarly tomorrow has not yet arrived. We have access to it through imagination, but how much can we really know of tomorrow? Even less than we can recall of yesterday. It pays to look back and to look ahead wisely, firmly rooted in the here and now. Otherwise we risk living with unlikely daydreams and falsehood. Happiness built on such illusions is insecure. It is unlikely to last.

Yesterday and Tomorrow.

Sit quietly and comfortably. Try to recall some events from yesterday in your own life. Were you paying close attention? How real did these events seem at the time? How real do they seem now, looking back? How real do they seem compared to the events of today so far? How real for you is this moment? Spend a few minutes considering this.

Now try to imagine some events of tomorrow. Begin with something routine. How exactly can you picture, hear, feel, even smell what might take place? How likely is it that you will imagine it correctly? Can you imagine the unexpected? Ask yourself honestly about this, but there is no need, unless you wish, to take up very much time.

Of course we expect the unexpected to occur from time to time in our lives, but we cannot imagine the form it will take. Even if we try, we are unable to predict events with any precision. Even if it were possible, how much time would we wish to spend forecasting the future and how much really living in the present? If we always knew what was about to happen, there would be no excitement, fun or creativity in our lives. This is not really what we would choose.

What we might choose would be a balance between the expected and the unexpected. People usually say they want life to be interesting, that they want to avoid boredom and stagnation. Change and challenge can, however, produce unpleasant emotional stress. What we require then is equanimity – deep-seated confidence, happiness and peace of mind. This will equip us to lead an interesting, even a demanding life. How are we to cultivate such excellent and helpful attributes? With application and concentration, with diligence and perseverance – with a good, whole bucket and with a long enough piece of rope.

Happy and Unhappy Emotions

8

People are different but the same,
The same but different!
We are especially alike in our feelings,
In our emotions.
When losses occur,
We feel sad. (H 91)

In some of us, according to our temperament and conditioning, the well of happiness is deeper beneath the surface than in others. When there are more layers of unhappinesss to be met, the rope and bucket must go down further to reach the water of joy and then bring it out of the darkness into the light of our conscious minds.

As we will see, it is not a question of avoiding painful emotions but of suffering them, of allowing, even of encouraging them to ripen and come to a natural state of completion.

How Many Emotions Can You Name?

Sit quietly in comfort for a few minutes. Let your mind settle.

Reflect upon your emotions and those of other people. See how many you can name. Use a piece of paper and write them down if you like. Spend as long as you want to on this.

Now, ask yourself, 'How many of these emotions do I experience in a day?' Are there any that you do not share with other people? Think about your list. Can you divide your emotions into 'pleasant' and 'unpleasant'? Which of the two lists is longer?

All our emotions are linked, and all our emotions link us to one another. We are brothers and sisters in a kind of communion of emotions. It pays us to understand them and to give them proper attention.

There are probably countless human experiences which can be called emotional, and we are likely to experience many of them in the course of one day. Usually, too, we take more notice of (and are better at naming) unpleasant rather than pleasant emotional experiences. This may be because our fundamental experience is pleasant. When any change occurs, when there is a moment of disequilibrium, we take notice – and feel this change as unpleasant. Such experiences are usually accompanied by thoughts like, 'I am uncomfortable, I feel bad. I do not like this. I do not want this experience. I wish it would stop'.

This is a characteristic of our everyday emotions. They are usually intimately related to certain kinds of thought, but we can avoid some of the confusion by listing some basic emotions that seem to exist before any thoughts get attached to them. It may be helpful to call them the 'rudiments' or 'archetypes' of everyday emotions. In the scheme that follows there are just eight of these, and they fit together something like the colours of the rainbow or the notes of a musical scale.

We have met a number of these emotions already, and will be looking at a fuller list in Chapter 15; but first, in introducing the eight rudimentary emotions of this spectrum or scale, we need to remember two things. One of these may come as a surprise. The other can seem to be a bit of a problem.

The surprise is that each rudimentary emotion comes in two forms: pleasant and unpleasant. The problem is a problem of language: we have a good set of names for the uncomfortable, unpleasant, unhappy or 'painful' forms, but fewer and less satisfactory names for the pleasant, happy or 'pain-free' forms.

It is also important for you to note that we are not going to use the words 'positive' and 'negative' in connection with emotions. This is primarily because unpleasant feelings can sometimes be useful, and we may see them as positive. For example, anxiety can alert us to a situation needing urgent action, and doubt may prompt us to seek out more information that we need. A descriptive word seems best in this context then, rather than one that implies an opinion or value judgement.

Confusion and Clarity.

Sit in comfort once more. If necessary, read these last few paragraphs again. Observe whether there is any confusion or bewilderment in your mind.

If you are feeling a little confused, *simply observe what the experience feels like, what thoughts arise with it and what impulses.*

For example, there may be an impulse for you to reject the complications and give up. If so, is the impulse to give up on the exercise, part of the chapter, the whole thing or even perhaps the whole book? If there are such feelings, try to be calm about them. You can have confidence that your mind will be able to sort itself out.

Now, try and remain focused on observing the feelings of bewilderment. Observe what happens to the thoughts and impulses when you concentrate on the feelings. Neither thoughts nor impulses can then have space to totally occupy your mind and will therefore tend to dissipate, no longer able to distract you. Concentrating on the feelings, which began by being unpleasant, observe what happens gradually to them. Watch them change, both in strength and character. Watch them ripening.

Alternatively, if you are not confused and all seems clear to you, note the clarity of your mind. Note how different clarity is from bewilderment – its opposite in fact.

Clarity is one of the experiences on the pleasant side of our basic rudimentary emotional spectrum. Spend a few moments reflecting on this now. See if it makes sense to you that as bewilderment increases, clarity decreases; also conversely that as bewilderment departs, clarity cannot help but be improved.

When bewilderment ripens fully within the mind, it turns into clarity. The same process happens with each of the eight basic emotions. They are in pairs. There are two forms and the unpleasant, unhappier form, when it is left undisturbed in the mind for long enough, dissipates. This process allows it naturally to become transformed into its more pleasant, happier partner.

When we observe how **painful** gradually matures into **pain-free** we begin to understand how every pathway of emotion can lead to happiness in the end. Every painful emotional experience can have a positive value for us, providing an opportunity for our individual and collective growth, for greater self-knowledge, for the development of equanimity and wisdom. This is how we can become more emotionally mature and discover how to be happy.

Matters of Faith and Belief 9

Happiness requires constant effort and vigilance.
It demands mindfulness,
Presence of mind. (H 96)

If you believe in something, you will have your reasons for doing so. Perhaps someone you trust has told you something, and you accept it because of your trust in that person. But what happens when two people, each of whom you trust, tell you different and conflicting things about something? What happens when you do not yourself have enough knowledge or experience to decide what to believe for yourself? This is where intuition and wisdom come in.

Patience and perseverance are necessary for progress in understanding the emotions, and eventually in mastering them. Patience and perseverance in turn require commitment, determination and faith. Faith is not quite the same as belief.

What You Trust and Believe.

Sit quietly and in comfort for a few minutes. Close your eyes if you wish.

Now, think about what you believe and how you have come to believe it. Think, for example, about the colours of the rainbow.

How many are there? Can you name them? How much of what you know depends on what you have been told, and how much on direct observation? How closely have you observed and taken in with your mind what you see with your eyes? When you look at a rainbow in the sky, which colour is uppermost, red or violet?

Now think about which you trust more, what people tell you or what you experience for yourself? How often do these seem to be in conflict?

Continue to think about these matters for as long as you wish, but then sit quietly for a little longer. Notice first whether this thinking has affected your emotional state, and in what way. Have you become a little confused or bewildered? Did you begin to experience any doubt? If so, watch this in your mind. Take up your good upright posture. Bring your mind back from your thoughts and emotions, back to the breath. Watch the breath for a few minutes and notice both thoughts and emotions settling down. Watch your emotions growing excited again whenever you recommence thinking.

Remain seated until you feel quite calm once again, and perhaps even notice yourself beginning to smile.

It seems worthwhile for each of us to try and reason some things out for ourselves. In doing so, we often have to listen to others and learn from them, but it is right to trust our own direct observations. It is probably also right to question common sense at times, to develop and come to trust our own gradually improving and deepening intuition.

*

When the conditions of sunshine and rain are such that a rainbow appears, we can each verify its colours for ourselves. We may need to have been told their names: red, orange, yellow, green, blue, indigo and violet. We can also recognise our emotions from personal experience, but we may need help to name them.

Most people trust their own observations first and then what they are told. Problems tend to arise when the matter in hand is deemed by someone (or by everyone) to be particularly serious and weighty. The more something seems to matter, the more strongly we hold on to our associated set of beliefs.

This is an interesting turn of phrase. We 'hold' our beliefs. There is us and there are the beliefs, and the two are somehow attached. 'I believe this', means, 'I am attached to this belief'. Now the question emerges: 'How weak or strong is your attachment to this or that particular belief?'

A link can now be seen between beliefs and opinions. Many would accept that a strongly held opinion and a weakly held belief are much the same. In both cases, if you were concerned, you would have to admit to the possibility of doubt, to the *possibility* that what you said you believed was in fact not true – or at least not the whole truth. More information, in such a case, could either strengthen or weaken your opinion or belief.

Both opinions and beliefs are ideas. They are created and can exist only in our minds. Neither a lightly held opinion nor a fiercely held belief, neither can change fundamentally the way things are. No one, simply by thinking about it, could invent a new colour or make the rainbow turn upside down.

Faith, on the other hand, depends upon more than our intellect, our powers of observation and reasoning. It depends upon bringing together all of the faculties of the mind – senses, thoughts, emotions, impulses and consciousness – in a particular and creative way. We are then able to observe clearly by pure experience, in stillness and openness – openness of the senses, openness of mind, openness of the heart and openness to follow the impulses of faith (of 'wisdom') as opposed to the impulses of reason. Until you are accustomed to it, this degree of openness can be a little bit scary.

An Inspirational Place.

Sit quietly at home for a few moments and think first about a place where you might expect to find inspiration, perhaps somewhere familiar to you, a beauty spot, the seashore, an old or religious building for example. If you cannot think of such a place, your exercise now is to find one – by looking at maps and guide books or perhaps by going exploring.

When you have decided, go and visit that special place. Go alone. Either go in your mind's eye or, better still, plan a visit. If you can, make your visit today.

You may not have to travel far. The right place could be nearby, even an altar or shrine in your own home, or a place of peace and beauty in your garden. If so, be careful not to be distracted during your visit by such thoughts as, 'This place needs dusting', or, 'The grass could do with being cut'! Whenever this happens, it may be best to go elsewhere. If you do not find the right place immediately, try another. Why not keep a selection of alternatives ready in mind?

Now, in the right place – either in your mind or in reality – sit quietly and take it all in. Use all your senses. Shut your eyes to listen and smell. When you are ready, get up and move around (slowly). In a minute, open your eyes.

When you have taken your fill of the atmosphere, sit quietly again and give your mind time to clear.

Now, think for a moment about faith, about opinions and beliefs. Try and experience for yourself the distinctions between them. Ask yourself, 'What do I really believe?' Then ask, 'Why do I believe it'? Then ask, 'Are there things that I trust without really knowing why? What are they?' Take as long as you like over these questions. Carry them around with you to examine occasionally during the next day or two as well if you wish. These are questions that repay perseverance.

When we find ourselves trusting something without knowing why, it is often a sign of intuition, a sign of faith. True faith is naturally associated with peace of mind. This tranquillity itself tends to overcome and banish both doubt and bewilderment. By enhancing calmness and clarity, faith also serves to promote happiness.

Opinions and beliefs, on the other hand, because they are assembled from ideas about reality and not from direct and present-moment observations of reality, are more susceptible to threat. Because they are always vulnerable to challenge, in a subtle way they promote doubt and confusion.

In other words, opinions and beliefs can be overturned. Depending upon how strongly we are attached to them, this threat sets up conflict and a potentially powerful impulse to defend them. While the concept of belief implies the existence of doubt, faith somehow allows for doubt and incorporates it. Faith therefore affects our whole psychology, taking us beyond doubt into an almost incommunicably complete sense of certainty. True faith cannot be challenged, but neither can it be explained.

This may be a little difficult to follow so far. With patience and perseverance, we will see in the next chapter how questions of faith, belief and opinion affect our emotional life so intimately.

A Story of our Time from Long Ago

What brings happiness?
The absence of sorrow,
The absence of anger,
The absence of doubt,
The absence of shame. (H 100)

Many years ago, we thought the world was flat. This was then a matter of common sense, of common experience. We walked on flat ground, observed great flat sheets of water on the larger lakes and smaller seas. If the earth were not flat people and things would tend to fall off. Without thinking too deeply, this was probably the best explanation for how things seemed to be.

Without thinking too deeply here means without paying close enough attention to observable information. It means being selective as to what we take into account. And it also means avoiding possible alternative explanations for what has been observed. It means being content with partial knowledge, and therefore with false understanding. Unfortunately, then, it means the acceptance and perpetuation of ignorance.

The first step is to recognise the incomplete nature of one's knowledge and understanding. The next step is to pay closer attention, to expand one's observations and perhaps record them. Eventually a new and more complete explanation of the situation will emerge.

Surprisingly, this is not always a happy event for everyone concerned. This is because we are attached to our opinions and beliefs. We hold onto them whatever their content and this, of course, includes occasions when they are incomplete, when they are misjudged, even when they are plain wrong. The problem is that we do not know they are wrong, or are not willing to accept it. So, if your attachment to an opinion or belief is threatened or indeed overturned, by new evidence or simply because someone else asserts differently, there will be an emotional reaction. This is what interests us here.

The Earth is Flat.

Sit quietly and in comfort. Close your eyes if you wish.

Imagine yourself living in a time when people thought of the earth as flat. Ask yourself how likely you are to have accepted this idea as the truth? Suppose now that you did accept it as definite truth and you heard for the first time a report that someone else had discovered that the earth was really not flat but round. Might you be tempted to deny it and disagree vigorously? What emotions might be involved?

Now imagine yourself to be the same person later on. Someone takes you aside and explains the astronomical observations and calculations that lead conclusively to the truth that the world is round. How might you feel, particularly when you remember your earlier defence of what now appears to be false?

Now relax again. Think about how you know what shape the earth really is.

Most people who now know the planet Earth to be a sphere will have seen, and have been convinced by, a photograph of it taken from a spacecraft. Before this, though, its true shape was known for many centuries. None of this changes the experience we have of it, though, as essentially flat, or at least flat with oceans, valleys, hills and mountains. Things are complicated. We have to be able to think about the earth in two different ways at the same time. In our marvellous minds, we can do that. There does not need to be conflict. Steam and ice are different forms of water. We are perfectly capable of dealing with apparent contradictions like that, but initially we may feel some emotional and cognitive confusion.

So, let us examine a sequence of events and the emotional experiences that might arise when a strongly-held belief is challenged.

Living a long time ago, I believe that the earth is flat. A friend tells me of a report that it is not, that it is round. I become bewildered, confused. I do not like this. I find it unsettling. My first tendency is to deny it. My friend insists. He says the report includes astronomical data and measurements that prove it. I grow impatient with him and angry. We ask someone else, and she too has heard the news, and is inclined to believe it, but I cannot accept it. In my anger, I abuse the woman and threaten to strike at my friend. Others join in. Some say I am right, others that I am wrong. Some refuse to take sides and are abused by the rest for not having the courage to make up their minds one way or the other. Some say they want to wait until more is known or until official policy is changed. Some, and I am one of these, know that loyalty to that policy is a factor in what we believe (or at least in what we say we believe). At this moment I am therefore doubly confused. My loyalty to the official ruling order protects me. I begin to feel anxious that if I were to really change my belief about the shape of the earth, there could be unpleasant repercussions. These could include material losses: my job and my livelihood. I do not want this to happen, but neither do I wish to betray my true self.

Later, when I realise that the argument is not going to be resolved by an arguing crowd of relatively ill-informed people, I decide to go home. When I get there and begin to calm down, I am struck suddenly with shame at the thought of what I said to my friend, and guilt at trying to assault him. I want to put things right with him as soon as possible. Like a brother to me since childhood, his friendship is more important to me, I realise, than what I think I believe. So now I am ready to admit to myself that there could be some truth in his report. Thinking more clearly, I also realise that there is nothing anyone could say which would in fact change the shape of the world. So now I relax and begin to feel a little happier.

Are your Opinions your Own?

Sit quietly or go for a walk. Reflect again on what you believe and why you believe it. Ask yourself how much you tell yourself you believe because others say it is what they believe. Ask yourself how much your opinions are decided because you want to conform? Be truthful with yourself.

Spend as much time as you want to on this.

A number of emotions were involved in the scenario described above: bewilderment, aversion (dislike), anger, shame, guilt, later relaxation (calm), and eventually a measure of happiness. In this list there are some missing from the eightfold rudimentary double-set mentioned in Chapter Eight. It is time now to fill the gaps in the rainbow, leading us confidently on towards happiness and equanimity.

True Freedom 11

What else brings happiness?
The absence of bewilderment, of anxiety,
The absence of worry, of guilt, of self-blame,
The absence of desire, of wanting. (H 101)

The list of emotions at the end of the last chapter is completed by want and by sorrow.

One of the most difficult emotions to appreciate, because it seems to be with us all the time, is wanting, or desire. When we wake in the morning, we feel hungry and want something to eat, something to drink. When we have had enough, we want to stop eating and drinking. We want to get on with the day. We want this. We want that. We almost always want something. Because it is such a common feeling, one we are so used to, it can be hard to separate ourselves from it. But it is possible. To be free of want is to be truly free.

Want like this is not in itself usually considered painful. This is because food and drink are usually available close by and without too much effort. But this kind of emotional hunger and thirst quickly become intense and painful when the desired object is not available. As soon as the volume of want is turned up, even a little, we are forced to take notice. It is no longer just there in the background. Turn on the tap to fill the kettle and discover that no water is flowing. How might your emotions respond?

The first thing to recognise is that wanting something always implies not-wanting something. 'I want food', equally means, 'I do not want to remain hungry'. Wanting and not-wanting are reciprocal forms of want. They can be called 'desire' and 'aversion'. Also the reverse is true. 'I dislike the smell of dirty socks', means something like, 'I want clean socks every day'. This is a useful point to understand.

Wanting and Not Wanting.

Sit quietly in comfort. Wait until you are feeling calm. If you find yourself distracted, sit with a good posture, watching or counting your breath for a few minutes.

Now, when you are calm, reflect upon whether there is anything you want in this immediate moment. For example, you may want to move or stretch to get more comfortable. You may want to open a window or darken the room. You may want someone else near-by to stop making a loud noise so that you can concentrate better. You may find yourself wanting to think about something else.

There are many possible desires and impulses that could arise, and they may be of mild or much stronger intensity. When you have identified one, reflect on what you want and also on what – in the same context – you do not want. For example, 'I want that loud noise to stop' equates with, 'I do not want that noise to continue'.

In other instances a useful linking word is 'but': 'I want to stretch, but I do not want to move and disturb my concentration'. It should be possible for you to think of many examples like these. Can you think of any desires that are not linked to any aversions?

It is important in this exercise to focus on the present moment, on newly-formed wants, wishes, desires, impulses and the aversions which accompany them. We need to distinguish them from the longer-term aversions and desires that motivate us more consistently and continuously. These are the stronger attachments, the likes and dislikes, which underpin our deeper values.

If you are hungry and eat, your hunger will pass. If you are hungry for success, fame, power or wealth, it does not seem likely that you will be satisfied soon after breakfast. There is a qualitative difference between these short and longer-term types of wish or desire.

This may be one of the more difficult chapters in this book for some people, because it challenges some of the assumptions by which we normally live. The basic assumption which common sense supports, but which wisdom condemns, is: 'If I can always have what I want, I will always be happy'.

If we accept it at face value for the moment, we can easily see how a number of consequences seem to follow. For example, you might then assume: 'If I achieve success, fame, wealth and power, I am more likely to be able to have what I want whenever I want it'. And you might also think: 'I will be able to avoid or do away with anything I do not want or like'.

This is the perfect recipe, however, for your wants and desires to multiply without limit. They could easily grow well beyond anyone's capacity to achieve them all, and well beyond anyone's capacity to enjoy even those which could be obtained.

This is the perfect recipe for your list of dislikes to grow rapidly too, well beyond anyone's ability permanently to avoid them all. Thus the assumption about how to achieve happiness through getting what you want and avoiding what you don't want by means of success, fame, wealth and power, is a false one. Unhappily, it is an assumption that for many has grown into more than an opinion. It has become a most tightly-held belief.

Is Happiness the Same as Getting What You Want?

Sit quietly or if you wish go for a walk. Think about becoming suddenly much wealthier or more powerful. How would that affect your life? Be as honest as possible with yourself. How much would it simply allow you to indulge your likes and dislikes, your desires and aversions, your love and your hate? How much indeed might it fuel them?

Now, think about happiness. Is that the same thing as getting what you want? Think deeply about this. Take as long over it as you please. Take as long over it as you need. Think about happiness and its relationship to tranquillity, to an inner feeling of peace. How important for you is it that they should be connected? Or are you only happy by being excited?

It may be helpful for you to consider the distinction between our wishes, our wants, and our needs. We need sustenance, for example. Bread and milk will suffice, but we may want caviar and champagne. It pays to be clear about the difference between necessities and desires, and to distinguish between them carefully as often as possible.

To give another example, it is natural to wish to be free from physical pain, discomfort, injury and ill health. But this is another wish that can give rise to false assumptions, a wish rather than a need when it comes to being happy. It is possible, once you have achieved a certain degree of equanimity, to be contented – even happy – during illness or while experiencing pain. If you have not experienced this for yourself, you may well doubt the assertion.

Doubting the inevitability of physical ailments may fuel in you the desire for health and fitness, youth and beauty, even to the point of obsession. This, though, is a denial of nature. We need to accept and respect the truth that everyone is subject to injury, illness, ageing and eventually death.

The search for true happiness does not seek to deny or avoid this inevitability, but takes it fully into account. Wisdom dictates acceptance. It may all sound rather grim at first, but we are wise to face the fear and displeasure brought on by disease and weakness, to find a way through and not around them to happiness. This is one of the central themes of this book.

So, if getting what you want and avoiding what you do not want is not the secret of happiness, what is? The answer lies in the absence of want, the absence of desire and aversion. The answer then is contentment. But how may contentment be achieved in a world filled with sorrow? We will begin considering this big question in the next chapter.

Sadness – the Golden Gateway to Joy

12

Wherever you are, Sitting or standing,
Give up desire.
Wherever you are, Walking or lying down,
Give up sorrow. (H 112–3)

We are always sitting, standing, walking or lying down. If we include kneeling, squatting, climbing, running and so on, the point is made. Twenty-four hours a day during every activity we are to remain mindful and be aware constantly of the state of our emotions. If we want to increase our experience of happiness, this is the first part of a universal and timeless prescription.

Whenever we encounter a sense of lack, of want, of desire, of need, we are to let it go. Similarly, whenever we encounter sorrow, we are to let that go as well. But it is not easy to give up want or sorrow, or any of the other painful emotions: anxiety, bewilderment, doubt, shame, guilt and anger. Of course the bad feeling will not go away immediately, but our attachment to it can be reduced.

The solution to the riddle also has to do with how our painful emotions are linked with each other, and with their opposite or complementary forms. 'Letting go', as we shall see, does not mean actively to push an unpleasant feeling aside, but to allow it to follow its natural path and resolve into its opposite. Remember, 'to suffer' also means 'to allow'.

Paradoxically then, we are to be fully aware of and permit, even foster, the experience of our emotions without impeding them. This takes considerable practice and skill, especially as we are taught and encouraged to suppress painful feelings. Indeed, some of us are so accomplished at suppressing our emotions that others find it nearly impossible to tell much of the time what we are feeling. Only when the emotion is very powerful does an indication either of happiness or of distress break through what has become a kind of mask.

In some cases, we are unaware of our own emotional state, so unaccustomed are we to giving it attention, and so good are our powers of suppression. We will usually deny feelings that others suspect to be present in us. This applies especially to particular types of emotion.

For example, I may acknowledge a measure of guilt or anxiety from time to time, and you may deny ever feeling either. If you find uncertainty difficult to tolerate, you may strongly suppress experiences of both doubt and bewilderment. This, of course, can result in significant problems when long-cherished opinions or beliefs are challenged. We will return to this again later.

Postural Sensations.

Sit quietly in comfort, taking up a good upright posture. (You may find that a firm, upright chair is better for this than a softer, easier one.) Allow your thoughts and feelings to settle.

Now reflect on the actions and positions of your body throughout the twenty-four hours. On average, how much time do you spend each day sitting? How much time do you spend standing? How much time do you spend each in walking and lying down?

When you are sitting, standing, walking and lying down, how aware are you that this is what you are doing: 'Now I am sitting; now I am standing, etcetera'? How do you know which it is? How much does information from your body – from buttocks, feet, legs, torso, head and eyes – play a part?

Now pay attention to this for a few moments as you are sitting there. How do you know you are sitting? What are the physical sensations involved? If it helps you to focus your mind on information from the other senses, especially on the sense of touch, you may prefer to close your eyes.

Enjoy the sensations for as long as you wish, but there is no need to do it for too long.

For each of us, there are times when we feel sad. There is personal loss, and there are times when we are affected as members of groups and communities. The largest community includes the whole population of the world. Indeed, for some, this also includes all those people who have lived and died, as well as those who are yet to be born. Thus each day we have access to a collective sadness by identifying with others who are experiencing sometimes massive loss and destruction.

There are occasions for sorrow every day, but many of us deny frequent feelings of sadness. We may fleetingly feel something, minor irritation perhaps, when yet another natural disaster is reported in the media, but we have learned to protect ourselves from significant and disabling levels of distress by not engaging fully with the grief of others. There will also be times when, individually, we are unable to prevent sorrow being awakened within us. And there will be times when sorrow seems to affect us all.

12

Into the Well – Sadness.

Prepare yourself for this exercise. We are going deep into the well of life and death to taste genuine sorrow, our own sorrow. (You may prefer to have tissues nearby.)

In addition to sadness, other feelings may be aroused, such as anger and shame. Give yourself adequate time. Later you may need a while to recover. Above all, pace yourself. Do not let strong painful feelings overwhelm you. Also, it is important to try not to act on any painful feelings that arise. Wait for them to subside. Reassure yourself. We are going into the well, but we are also coming back out into the sunshine again.

You can do this either at home or in one of your special places, wherever you feel comfortable and in harmony with your surroundings. Sit quietly and spend a few moments watching your breath until you feel quite still and calm.

Now, once you are calm and still, think about sorrow. Wait and see if any personal sadness comes to mind. If so, allow your mind to explore this, trying to remain in contact with the sad feelings.

If no example of personal sorrow comes to mind at the start of this exercise, there are a number of ways in which the experience may be prompted. This means using your imagination to invent or recall a sad occasion and really engage with it. Sit quietly and attempt this. You may recall the death of a prominent and well-loved person, for example. You may find it helpful to look at photographs, listen to evocative music, watch videotape recordings of sad events such as natural disasters affecting the innocent, particularly children.

Most of us, when we are sad, simply want the experience to stop and become preoccupied with thoughts about when it will stop. When it does not seem to be stopping, we may begin to grow anxious or angry. If your sorrow does begin to give way to other emotions or to excessive verbal thoughts and questioning, stop and focus again on your breathing. When calm again, return to feelings of sorrow.

While you are experiencing the effects of sorrow, concentrate on the physical sensations and experiences that characterise it. Usually, this means tears. Crying and tearfulness are the hallmarks of sorrow. When distress is severe, sobbing may also start. As well as the eyes and nose, the lungs and diaphragm get involved, their movements becoming jerky, losing their rhythm, and involuntarily setting off the vocal cords too. See how much of this is happening to you as you focus your mind on your sadness.

Now, try to be a neutral observer of your sorrow, at least for a moment. Does observing it neutrally without wishing it to stop affect the experience? Ask yourself in what way.

Take as long as you need over this exercise to engage with the feelings of sadness. When you are ready, focus again on your breathing and let the painful experiences fade out. Open your eyes. Look around you. Come back to the present moment. Sit quietly until you regain equilibrium, until you feel calm and happy again.[6]

Now, take stock of yourself. For some, it will have been a surprise to discover strong feelings. You may want to talk to a friend or loved one about your experiences. You may also benefit from repeating the exercise from time to time, bringing intense calm and stillness face to face with your sadness to soften it. In time, even deep-seated sadnesses pass. Rest now in tranquillity for a few moments longer.

[6] If painful and troubling emotional experiences persist or become severe, do not hesitate to seek advice and assistance. You will not be alone. It is best to be honest with yourself about it. Talk to family and friends. If necessary, call on your family doctor or seek professional counselling. Also check out the resources at the end of this book (p. 203–8). There is no blame or shame in asking for help. In fact, it is the mature thing to do.

If you have not been able to locate any sadness within your own mind during this exercise, and are therefore tempted to think it was a failure or a waste of time, ask yourself, 'Am I truly happy?' If the truthful answer is 'Yes', that is terrific, but if it is not, you may find that it is anger, or some other unhappy emotion, which currently blocks your experience of sorrow. (You may benefit from trying the exercise again, focussing on anger this time instead of sadness.) We are going to discuss this point in more detail later on.

This is a difficult exercise. It is real work, hard work, work on yourself. But its usefulness cannot be underestimated. Getting in touch with your sorrow, albeit a painful and distressing process, is to reach down towards the source of the genuine waters of happiness. Here we have one of the golden gateways to joy.

Crying releases dammed-up emotional energy and allows a re-stabilisation of the emotional system. It is part of what is called a 'catharsis' (from the Greek word which means 'cleansing'). Another form of emotional catharsis is laughter, but we must look more closely at sadness before we are quite ready for fun.

Avoidance of Grief – the Rogers' Story

13

Sorrow, crying, tears . . . resolution!
The mind starts healing itself. (B 27)

We have to go to the bottom of the well, to go through all the layers of emotional pain, before healing can begin. There are no exercises in this chapter, only a true story. After reading it, those who wish to can try and imagine what it would have been like to be involved. Try to experience the feelings of each of the participants in turn, as a way of gaining some insight into emotional pain and recovery.

*

David and Carol Rogers,[7] both hardworking people in their early forties, were the parents of three children. The youngest, Lucy, had diabetes. She was ten years old. The oldest, Stephen, had learning difficulties. He was almost sixteen. In between was Chrissie who, at fourteen, was helpful by nature, quiet and intelligent.

A few years before the story begins, when Lucy first became unwell with the diabetes, she had collapsed one day and had been taken to the nearby children's hospital. The family did not let Stephen visit her there, for fear that he would have become disruptive. David stayed at home with him, but left him once each day to take Chrissie to visit

---

[7] The names of everyone throughout the book have been changed.

both Lucy and Carol, who was staying in the hospital with her daughter. It was a worrying time. Lucy was precious. Each member of the family secretly feared losing her; but no one mentioned this. Their irrational fear was that to speak about something awful might make it happen.

Once the doctors had made a diagnosis, and they had had the illness and its treatment explained to them, David and Carol felt easier. They were told, 'As long as Lucy takes her insulin regularly, everything will be all right'. This was what they believed.

Lucy did indeed get better quite quickly and soon went home. She submitted hesitantly to the insulin injections, which Carol gave her every day as she had been taught to by the hospital nurses. The only difference in the family seemed to be that Stephen became more irritable and impatient than usual.

Lucy had regular outpatient visits to the hospital, and was soon being told that she should learn how to give herself her insulin injections. It took a long time to coax her. She also found the diabetic diet hard to adhere to. She liked sweet things and chocolate. Her blood sugar levels went up and down, sometimes dangerously. On several occasions her condition deteriorated to the point where she needed to return to hospital for stabilisation. Surprisingly, once there her sugar levels quickly returned to and remained normal. Back at home they equally quickly went haywire again.

The hospital staff began to suspect psychological problems in the family. Lucy and her mother were referred to a counsellor, Mrs Hayes, who, after a couple of assessment sessions, decided to interview David as well. She also saw Chrissie once, but she did not ask to see Stephen.

Lucy's diabetes got worse. She began spending more and more time in hospital. Carol was unable to take any extra time off work, but used to visit, sometimes with Chrissie, sometimes with David, every evening. Only once did Stephen go with them, and on that occasion he stayed far away from his sister, appearing disinterested. When she next came home, he began to be repeatedly unkind to her. In addition, he started going out unaccompanied and staying out late. Sometimes when he returned, he seemed to have been drinking. Once he was arrested for shoplifting and given a warning. David took him to task more than once, but Stephen grew angry with him in return. Once it looked as if he might hit his father, but then he turned and ran off, staying out most of the night.

Soon Stephen was regularly calling his parents and his sisters cruel names, often swearing and threatening them verbally. It became a daily occurrence. He seemed permanently angry, and everyone was soon angry with him in return. Lucy's diabetes control remained poor and Chrissie's schoolwork suffered. Carol began to criticise her husband for failing to control their son's bad behaviour. David in turn, resenting this, began to spend more time with his friends. The family was quickly in crisis.

*

One day Carol went to see Mrs Hayes on her own and told her about the situation, revealing her own frustration and weariness as she did so. She felt that without her husband's support she was left to take responsibility for everything on her own. She did not let on how worried she was about Lucy's continuing deterioration.

Understandably, Mrs Hayes thought that the real problem in the family was Stephen. In her opinion, he was the one who now needed counselling to control his unreasonable and destructive behaviour. Before he started to become angry, the family seemed to be coping. She did not say so at first, but she was thinking that Stephen might even need to be removed from the family to some kind of special residential care. She decided to ask for more help and contacted a specialist family therapist.

*

After the therapist had been given details of the story, he agreed to see and assess the family, asking Mrs Hayes to come along as well. They all arrived together in her large people-carrier vehicle. Once inside the therapy room, the family arranged themselves in chairs in a semi-circle. Lucy sat between her parents, with Chrissie on the other side of her mother. Next came Stephen, and then Mrs Hayes between him and the therapist, who began by asking who wanted to tell him their story and why Mrs Hayes had asked them to see him.

After a lengthy silence it was Carol who spoke up. 'It's Stephen,' she said, pointing at him. 'We just can't control him any more. He is wearing us all out'.

It was a long session. Everyone had their chance to tell their version of what had been happening, why they thought it was happening and what to try next to make things better.

At first, Stephen was the main focus. Later the strain in the relationship between Carol and David became more evident. Only with direct prompting could the family be encouraged to discuss Lucy's illness as a possible contributing factor in their continuing problems and distress. The one who spoke most directly, genuinely and movingly about this, despite his learning difficulties, was Stephen. The therapist also noticed that he had to protect Stephen from interruptions by the others when he spoke. They were still angry, and had more or less stopped listening to him. The therapist gently pointed out that Stephen had something to say, and asked them to try and understand – and to help him understand – what it was that Stephen was trying to convey. 'He is trying to give us a message,' were his words. 'Let us all try and listen to what Stephen has to say.'

Stephen had been devoted to his younger sister at the onset of her illness. More than anyone, it turned out, he realised that she could die. While he knew this, everyone around him was concentrating on Lucy's recovery and on keeping her well. There was a kind of denial of the potential severity of the disease in her case. Carol and David's belief, 'As long as Lucy takes her insulin regularly, everything will be all right', was probably but not definitely and incontrovertibly true. The worse Lucy's condition became, the more often she had to go into hospital, the greater the threat of her eventually perishing seemed to become. Stephen knew this intuitively, and was by now finding it easier to get angry or to stay completely apart from her than to deal with the strong emotions involved.

Another factor was Lucy's apparent failure to comply with her insulin regime and her diet. Her parents were sympathetic and made excuses for her, but with a negative outcome. The nurses in the hospital, being naturally stricter, found it easier to restrict Lucy's bad eating habits and make her give herself her injections. Being sympathetic and lenient, although ultimately counter-productive, seemed easier to

David and Carol than admitting to themselves how serious the illness was, and therefore how necessary it was to be strict.

At the back of their minds, however, and harder to ignore as time went by and Lucy got worse, was the idea that Lucy could do more for herself, without being prompted and cajoled by others, in trying to control her diet and take her treatment. The temptation was to complain and get angry with Lucy herself, but for her parents this would have been unacceptable. It did not seem right to show anger towards their daughter whom they loved because she happened to have a potentially fatal illness through no fault of her own. So when Stephen got angry with Lucy, Carol in particular felt both ashamed and angry with him.

*

Much of this, and more, came out in the course of that one long morning session with the therapist. Eventually he asked everyone to be quiet and still for a moment as he asked them to think about Lucy, and for Lucy to think about herself, while imagining her back in the hospital that first time when everyone thought she might die. 'This, I think, is where all these bad feelings come from. This diabetes has not happened just to Lucy, whom you all love. It has deeply affected you all. Stephen has reacted differently, but he is not the major problem here. It is Lucy's illness, which the doctors and nurses cannot cure, and which so far Lucy has not been able to control on her own. Let us just think about this for a few minutes more.'

The mood in the room grew sombre. Nobody spoke for several minutes. Finally the therapist thanked them all for coming, saying they had made a good start and he looked forward to their next visit. He and Mrs Hayes then arranged a follow-up meeting. Eventually the family left with muted farewells, unaware that everything between them had changed.

*

It had been planned that Mrs Hayes would see the Rogers family again after just one week. Soon after their meeting she telephoned the therapist. 'I am so pleased and so grateful,' she began. 'There has been a complete change for the better – so much so that we may not even need to come and see you again.'

Mrs Hayes described the journey home after the initial session with the therapist. She said every member of the family was in tears. 'It was as if they had been to a funeral,' she said, adding after a pause, 'But it was good. I had a feeling these were tears that had needed to be shed for a long time.'

The Rogers family had returned for Mrs Hayes' session a week later much calmer, all of them smiling. Stephen had lost his anger and become helpful around the house like his sister, Chrissie. He liked feeling included once more and appreciated. Lucy had asked to see the nurse at the hospital for another lesson on giving herself insulin. This time she paid more attention than previously, and as she gave herself her next injection, she told her mother that somehow she was no longer afraid. She had also cut down on chocolate and sweets. Chrissie enjoyed having Stephen assist her with chores for her mother, and also appreciated the extra time freed up to spend studying for forthcoming exams. Finally, David and Carol were just beginning to be able to relax. One evening they had gone out for a walk together and had had a long talk.

*

The session with the therapist had enabled all members of this family to go right down to the bottom of the well of their pain. In fact it was Stephen who had been leading them there. The important thing for us to notice is that the release of painful feelings, the catharsis, had enabled a real and lasting change to occur. Lucy's illness was no different, but everyone's attitude towards it had changed. They were less resistant to it, less afraid of its possible consequences. They were better able to accommodate the demands – both practical and emotional – it placed on them. A great deal of energy that had been lost on worry, on holding on to false hope and on a kind of denial, was now available to them again for more constructive and pleasurable purposes. In a word, they were happier – and they were all more mature.

*

Therapeutic encounters are not always as swift and successful as that of the Rogers family. Once shown the way, it had taken honesty and courage on their part – the honesty to look directly at a real and serious threat, and the courage to experience the full force of the painful emotions engendered. In other words it had taken a long enough rope to go deep down to the bottom, to the true source of the threatened loss, and the good, unbroken bucket (or, as we might say, 'bottle') to contain those painful feelings securely while they sorted themselves out and resolved. Only unacknowledged and unspoken anxiety, together with the much more evident anger, had been in the way. Once exposed, these feelings lost their power and, once the catharsis had occurred, happiness was restored. We will look at this more closely, and think about the Rogers family again, in Chapter 17.

Joyful, Peaceful, Mindful Mind

14

Happiness depends on a clear mind,
Like the still, reflecting surface of a lake,
A lake on which there is no ripple of hatred,
And not a breath of desire.
That is all. (H 49)

In this chapter we will begin by returning briefly to expand on some of the points made earlier, especially in Chapter 2. It will help if we use the word 'Happiness' as a blanket term to cover all the eight pleasant emotions in the basic set. Central to this book is the idea that happiness depends upon an undistracted mind, on a mind that is still and clear.

As we cultivate stillness and clarity in our minds, we encounter a deep intuition, quite distinct from common sense, free of worldly conditioning. This intuition is a kind of knowledge that is already somehow dwelling within us, in our hearts and minds. Some would call this sacred knowledge or wisdom. Some would call it our birthright.

In order to reach and benefit from this intuitive knowledge, we need to master our minds, because we have access to it through stillness and silence. Sitting quietly with consciousness focused on the present moment for five, ten or twenty minutes once or twice a day is therefore highly recommended. This joyful and peaceful discipline can be described as a spiritual practice.

Sit quietly in this way in silence, with the mind respectfully focused on itself in the immediacy of the here and now, and it may at first seem to you pointless, boring and dull. With practice, however, remarkable things can happen that carry inevitable benefits for our everyday life.

*

Happiness has several identifiable emotional components. What are they? Obviously joy, joyfulness, is one of these. If this is so, then sadness, its complementary form, will be absent. Although it is true that joy and sadness are often experienced as mingled or rapidly alternating in sequence, we can separate and distinguish them. This is obvious because joy feels quite different from sadness and we know that sorrow is incompatible with happiness in its purest form. We will look more closely at the simple emotions that make up happiness, and consider the opposites of each that must be absent for it to be (if possible) perfect. Pure or perfect feelings are rare but they contribute to everyday emotions in a way we are going to try to clarify.

*

There are many words in English for similar emotional experiences. Some of them distinguish mainly between different intensities of a given feeling. 'Irritation' is a relatively mild form of anger, for example, compared with 'rage', which is much stronger.

Most everyday emotional experiences are complex or composites. This means that two or more of the pure forms from the basic rudimentary set are involved, sometimes in both pleasant and painful forms, more or less simultaneously. Take, for instance, 'ambivalence'.

This means feeling good about something and feeling bad about it in more or less equal measure at the same time. It is a subtle form of want – wanting something and not wanting it at the same time. As such, doubt is usually also part of the experience, plus frequently a measure of bewilderment, possibly anxiety.

This is a 'Catch-22'. When we feel ambivalent, satisfaction – getting what we want – is hard to achieve. Because it often arises when we fail to get satisfaction, anger is therefore frequently also involved. The way out of ambivalence is to change yourself, to change the way you feel by changing what you want. Indeed there is a memorable expression – 'I want to be free more than I want what I want' – which can help you shift the focus of your desire, enabling a more speedy return to happiness and inner peace.

Inner calm, peace, tranquillity – this feeling is another key component of happiness. It arises naturally, as distractions subside, during those periods of sitting quietly. This deeply-rooted inner calm is the pivot-point of equanimity. It protects us against its converse, a sense of threat, feelings of anxiety. Calm and gladness go together. Both are central to our happiness.

Anxiety disturbs tranquillity. You cannot remain calm when you feel under any kind of threat. The tendency is to worry, which implies a measure of uncertainty and also bewilderment. To understand how a sense of threat arises, we must look again at desire, at want and not-wanting. This will also help us later understand anger.

*

Want, in its purest or rudimentary form, has no object. It is a stand-alone feeling like hunger might be when there is no food available.

14

As soon as an object comes into mind, however, simple wanting becomes the everyday experience of desire. Desire always has an object. We always desire something. And this distinction holds for all emotions. We can be non-specifically anxious, angry or sad for no reason, and these are the basic rudimentary feelings. But in everyday life we are usually anxious, angry or sad about something or with someone.

There is of course no end to the possible objects of our emotions. There is no limit to the range of physical objects, animals, plants, people, ideas and ideologies to which we may become attached, averse or ambivalent. And there are, of course, many gradations of attachment and aversion, desire and repulsion. These are factors in the richness and changeability of our emotional experience from moment to moment, as so many of these complicated positive and negative attractions are called into play.

The softest level of desire is perhaps indicated by words like 'whim' and 'fancy'. These are slight wishes or inclinations. For stronger levels of desire we use words like 'craving' and 'passion', even 'addiction'. Unfulfilled craving or addiction is extremely unpleasant, a severe form of human suffering, implying that any satisfaction would be short-lived and soon give way to more craving. But the converse of desire is not aversion, for this is another form of want which gives rise to equal or greater levels of suffering at times. Intense aversion, extreme dislike, is what we refer to as 'hatred'. Note how close this is to intolerance, anger, aggression, destruction, brutality – possibly to the most pervasive and intense form of painful human suffering in the world.

*

The true converse of desire and of aversion is contentment. This is the emotional experience that depends on the absence of desire, on the absence of likes and dislikes within the mind.

At first thought, it may seem impossible to achieve. Everyone is subject to a wide range of likes and dislikes. This is normal. But it is a question of seeing through them and of somehow going beyond them. And the key to success in this depends once more upon our ability to master our minds and learn how to maintain our mental focus on the present moment, in the here and now.

A mind centred on what is happening within itself in the present moment, taking account of sense perceptions, thoughts, emotions and impulses – as well as on intuition from the inmost well-spring of wisdom – will not be distracted by desire, by likes and dislikes, by whims and wishes, passion and craving. It will already be full. Full of what? Full of joy – joyful. Full of peace – peaceful. Full of itself – mindful. It will be empty of painful emotions.

That is why sitting patiently in silence, attentive to the mind itself, is recommended. This allows us to simmer down and rest, to let go of destructive desires and preoccupations, to heal and to mature. It allows us, as everybody deserves, to be happy.

Happiness is our birthright.

Staying in Focus: Watch your Breath, or Repeat a Mantra.

Sit quietly now. Take up a good upright posture. Close or almost close your eyes. Bring your mind gently to focus on the present, on the here and now. Watch your breath, breathing inward and outward. Focus on the abdomen or the nostrils – decide which. Whenever you become distracted, gently return the mind to the present each time. If you have problems holding your concentration, it may help to count each breath. Count each in-breath up to four and then begin counting again.

If you still have problems with your concentration, try repeating a suitable word or phrase as you breathe in and out, in rhythm with your breathing. For example repeat the phrase, 'May I be well', on the in-breath and, 'May others be well', on the out-breath.

(A word or phrase used in this way is called a mantra. The word 'mantra' can be translated as 'mind-protector', because it is used to protect or guard your mind against distractions and negative thoughts. If you cannot think of an uplifting word or phrase for yourself, you could simply use, 'Good Day'. Or you may prefer this reminder-phrase to have a more directly spiritual connection.[8] There is no reason for you not to choose your own word or phrase.)

Continue this practice for five, ten or twenty minutes, up to one hour (but no longer than that) each time. Hope to experience utter stillness of the mind, but also be warned against trying too hard to achieve anything.

[8] Christians, for example, might use a phrase like 'Hail, Mary', or perhaps one from The Lord's Prayer such as, 'Our Father', or 'Thy Will Be Done', or again simply an affirmative word like, 'Amen', which means 'So be it'. The Hindu word invoking the highest Godhead, 'OM' (pronounced or intoned as a triple sound – oh, ooh, mmm), is commonly used by people of that and other religious traditions. A Hebrew word that many might equally prefer is 'Shalom', which means 'Peace'.

A mind that is clear is free of bewilderment. This clarity is the basis of knowing, of wisdom, of certainty, of confidence, ultimately of faith.

A mind that knows, a sure mind dwelling in the present, lacks nothing. Free of doubt, it feels whole, complete, full, and contented. Because desire and aversion are absent, this mind is calm, tranquil, at peace. Because it is at peace, it accepts everything, resists nothing, and so is free of anger. Free of anger and desire, it is free too of shame and guilt. Free of attachment to anything except the ever-changing present, it holds to nothing and wants nothing. Holding to nothing, fearing no threat, it is free of anxiety. Holding to nothing yet lacking nothing, contented, fearing no loss, there is no cause within it for sorrow. Thus the mind free of sorrow is joyful.

This mind, the mind of happiness, is clear, content, sure, worthy, innocent, kind, calm and joyful. It is free of desire, aversion, bewilderment, doubt, shame, guilt, anger, anxiety and sadness. How can we discover this mind within ourselves and make it our everyday mind? We can find it with practice and perseverance, but also by developing our understanding of these emotions and their inescapable inter-connectedness.

*

It is necessary to distinguish the basic, pure, rudimentary emotions, the eightfold double set (see p. 96), from the emotional experiences of everyday life. It may seem like more of a theoretical distinction than a real one, but it can be useful nevertheless. To put it simply, rudimentary emotions stand alone. Everyday emotions arise in context.

This means that while you are sitting in silence and solitude, as in some of the exercises practised earlier, an emotional experience may simply arise in the mind, a feeling of sadness say, for no obvious reason. It may be a fleeting experience, only a slight sensation, but it is clear and pure enough to give a name to. You are not sad *about* anything at that moment, you are simply sad.

In everyday life, our emotions change continuously. They change in nature and in strength, sometimes with mercurial rapidity. As we discussed in Chapter 5, in ordinary life our emotions are not divorced from sense perceptions, thoughts, impulses and actions. They are all intimately and seamlessly linked. Facial expressions and automatic gestures, for the most part under unconscious control, bear expressive witness to this.

Emotional feelings are largely made up of subtle changing inner bodily sensations, for example a prickling feeling around the eyes when we are sad, warmth in the cheeks when we feel ashamed or embarrassed. Thoughts can bring on particular emotions, and always influence them. Likewise, emotions can initiate thoughts, and may give them added colour or flavour.

It is not essential for you to master all the points made in this and the following chapter. Some of them are difficult, especially if unfamiliar, but they are likely to become clearer as we proceed. If you are feeling confused, it is best not to struggle too hard with these ideas, but don't give up on them altogether. Confused thoughts are associated with the emotional state of bewilderment, and it is often necessary for us to go through this stage on our way to understanding and wisdom. Indeed, as we are about to see, we have to go through and beyond *all* the painful emotions.

The Full Rainbow of Emotion

Anxiety, bewilderment, wanting, anger,
Doubt, guilt, sorrow and shame.
These emotions often trouble the mind. (H 84)

In describing our emotions, we face a problem of vocabulary. When 'want', for example, is experienced in a pure and gentle form, what is that like for us? How do we find accurate words to describe the experience?

Sadness is a common feeling, one that most of us will recognise easily. We do not need to identify the immediate cause of our sadness. Where want is concerned, however, it is easier for us to recognise it in the context of *wanting something*. But there are words we can use to express it in a purer form, like 'hunger', 'thirst' and perhaps 'loneliness'. For example, it is common to feel want, on its own or coupled with bewilderment, in certain stages, for example, of grief, especially as we emerge from the initial feelings of numbness and shock.

The list below will help us as we set out to explore these ideas about pure forms of emotion. See it perhaps as a tool with which to begin the process, a firm basis for further enquiry.

The Eightfold Set of Basic Rudimentary Emotions

Pain-free	Painful
Clear-minded	Bewildered
Contented	Wanting
Sure	Doubtful
Worthy (virtuous)	Ashamed
Innocent	Guilty
Kind (accepting)	Angry
Calm	Anxious
Joyful	Sad

It is often difficult to disentangle an emotion from associated bodily sensations, actions and thoughts. For example, 'I hate the smell of sour milk!', is a thought about an emotion – extreme dislike, hate, aversion – which expresses that emotion, but is not far away from the emotion itself. We may well mentally conjure up the feeling of distaste in order to describe it. The same or similar emotion may also arise in the listener, as a sympathetic reaction.

So we begin by developing this short list of those emotions that seem fundamental. Using the comprehensive eightfold double set as building blocks, it should theoretically be possible to create all the rest of our feelings. In order to do so, we will first need to explore the interrelationship between the eight rudimentary emotions, to see how they fit together as a healthy system, geared not only to resolution and equanimity but also to gradually evolving emotional resilience and maturity.

15

Observing Emotions. Enjoy the Calm. Enjoy the Clarity.

Sit quietly with an upright posture. Watch your breath. Spend five minutes or more doing this. If you notice any emotions arise, however gently, simply observe them, feel them, experience them, perhaps just giving them their name in the silence of your mind.

If you are feeling happy, feeling good, rest in that joy. If you are not, watch (or count) your breath. If you are very distracted, try walking up and down, or in a circle. Watch your footsteps, one by one. Experience the sensation of your feet in contact with the carpet or the grass, and the rhythmical movements of your limbs.

Gradually, experience your mind settling down. Be patient. Eventually, as you become calm, a smile will appear on your face. Enjoy the calm. Enjoy the smile. Enjoy the clarity of your mind.

Take as long over this as you wish. Carefully notice any distractions or disturbances, either from outside you or from within your own mind. Notice them. Be patient. Do not grasp hold of them. Let them go. If you can, let them simply pass by. If you cannot, return your thoughts to your breath, to your reminder-phrase (your mind-guard or mantra) or to awareness of your feet on the ground.

Now, once more, enjoy the calm. Enjoy feeling the warmth of your smile. Enjoy feeling good about yourself. Enjoy the happiness. Let it last. It does not last forever. Let it simply last as long as it lasts.

Now, when you are seated again and your mind is still, use your imagination to explore the idea of want as an emotion. Can you identify it? It is subtle. Do not worry if you cannot. Can you identify bewilderment as you try to experience wanting? If so, explore this in your mind and your imagination.

Now, can you identify the form of want that is not-wanting? (When mild this is a subtle kind of defensive feeling. When strong it is one of outright rejection, even repulsion.) Continue to explore these feelings for a while, then bring your mind gently back to focus once more on your breathing. Take your time. Allow long enough for your emotions to settle again and your mind to become clear.

Eventually, when you are ready, please go back to your life.

'I am okay.' 'I feel good.' 'I am happy.' 'I feel fine.' These are short sentences you might use when experiencing emotional well-being. As we have seen 'happiness' can cover, more or less completely, this all-encompassing state. It is not ideal, because the same word can be used to refer to just one of the eightfold range of pleasant emotions – joy – as well as all of them together.

Usually we spend very little time analysing pleasant feelings in this way. We pay more attention to, think and worry about, bad feelings rather than good ones. Perhaps this is because these are the ones we want to change. It is also natural to be concerned that if we were to pay more attention to feeling good, we might then start thinking about the possibility of losing the good feeling and become anxious. In other words, we might begin to feel bad.

Why do we not dwell on our good feelings? As well as being fearful that they might evaporate, is there not also the sense – perhaps quite a subtle sense – that feeling good is our usual or 'meant to be' condition? We are not meant to think about it much, but just to enjoy it.

Wisely, this attitude accepts that good feelings do not last indefinitely. While they are present, there is an opportunity for us to benefit in terms of action. There is energy and optimism present, so that deeds can be done and things can be achieved. Sometimes, therefore, when we just sit or walk around feeling good, we worry that we might be thought of as lazy. But this is worth challenging. It may not really be part of human nature, but an unfortunate value judgement that has arisen as part of our cultural conditioning. Why is it unfortunate? Because if we have been taught to feel even a small measure of discomfort or shame when we experience happiness (especially, say, in the face of another's misery or distress) our joy cannot be pure and complete; it must be mixed with pain. We will need to think fairly deeply about this again later on.

How to be happy spontaneously is something many of us knew about in childhood that we have to re-learn later on. Our propensity for guilt and shame have come to dominate feelings of innocence and self-confidence. Our task is to rediscover how to be happy without immediately starting to feel anxious, ashamed, guilty or bad in some other way.

This, in a sense, is a fundamental problem with painful human emotion. It is natural at different times for both pleasant and unpleasant feelings to arise. Sometimes we feel good and sometimes we feel bad. This is not the problem. The essential problem is that when we feel bad we may in addition feel bad about that. Even when we feel good, we can also sometimes feel bad about it. Thus the problem is not only that we have emotional feelings, but that we have feelings about our feelings as well.

This is one of three main sources of persistent and problematic unhappiness in our lives.

Feelings about feelings represent one source of emotional problem. Thoughts about feelings represent another, and actions (or simple impulses) arising from feelings represent the third. We will come back to this in a later chapter. Now we will try and focus mainly on happiness, on feeling good.

*

Arguably we take emotional well-being for granted because it is our natural state. For the most part we feel good about feeling good so it causes us no problems. We do not need to think about it.

Perhaps it is like this. On a day when a fair wind is blowing, you are standing on a hillside. Your hair and clothing are blown about, as are things around you, leaves on the trees, loose pieces of paper and so on. There is a sensation on your cheeks and maybe too a smarting and watering in your eyes. If the wind is very strong, you have to lean into it to stay upright – and this requires both effort and a sense of balance. But if you were to look up on such a day, you might see a hot-air balloon gliding gently by overhead. For people in that balloon, as you can imagine, the experience of the wind – the same wind – will be different. Moving ahead of it in the balloon, they will not be experiencing the force of it. Because they are moving along with the wind, at its pace, the air about them is more or less still. They are not being buffeted. Their ride is both smooth and calm. In order to contain and control your emotional reactions and go with the flow of events, it may be useful to bear this allegory in mind. It is hard to control events. It is definitely easier to control our emotions.

Enjoying a Drink and Reflecting on Happy Emotions.

Make yourself a cup of your favourite warm drink: tea, coffee or cocoa perhaps. If it is a hot day and you would prefer, get yourself a cold drink – water, apple juice, iced lemon, whatever you like. Take your time over preparing or fetching it. Pay attention. Make it with care. Focus on what you are doing, something for yourself.

Now take your drink and sit down quietly, alone. Hold the cup in both hands and feel it, feel the cool or the warmth. Smell it. Smell the aroma. When it is no longer too hot, or before it has started to grow warm, take a sip. Taste the drink, really taste it. Let your mind dwell on these sensations: touch, temperature, smell, taste.

When you have finished the drink, set your cup or glass aside but remain where you are. Remain sitting. Be still.

In the same way that a moment ago you were exploring your sensory experiences, explore now the state of your emotions. Are you feeling happy, contented? Enjoy the feeling for a while. Rest in your contentment.

15

Now, if you feel calm and your mind seems clear, spend a few minutes reflecting on the list of emotions on p. 96. Try to see them as part of a double rainbow, or a kind of double musical scale. Concentrate first on the pleasant feelings listed, and consider how closely inter-related they are. Try to see whether they seem to make up the whole emotional composition or picture of what happiness is and can be for you. Can you think of any missing emotions?

Now, try to recall a time and place where you experienced a state of happiness involving all eight of these components. Explore this happy time in your mind's eye. Did love come into it somehow? Spend as long as you like over this part. You may find it helpful to make notes or write down a full account of this happy episode. You can use it as a resource to return to when things are perhaps not going so well. You may also want to tell someone about it later. Happiness is often better when you share it with someone close to you.

When you are ready, return quietly to the here and now. Reflect either on the warmth and sustenance of that hot drink, and the warm, happy contentment it gave you, or on the clear coolness of that cold drink, and the calm, tranquil clarity it restored. Drink up these feelings of gladness and calm while they last.

And if you were unhappy this time, if the exercise was not a success, simply return to it and try again another day.

Now, when you are ready, please return to your life.

It is sometimes difficult for us to find adequate words for pleasant emotional experiences. It is more difficult to differentiate the various elements of feeling happy than those of feeling unhappy. There is relaxed (or tranquil, or calm) and joyful (or elated, or glad), the opposites respectively of feeling anxious and sad. The converse of confused or bewildered is clear-minded or possibly 'enlightened'. But what of shame, doubt and guilt? The words we use do not immediately seem to refer to emotions – words like unashamed, certain and pure. These are not words we tend to use to identify feelings within ourselves. They are more like words that you would use to describe another person.

And here is a difficult question. What is the opposite of anger? What is the emotional state of someone who is, at least for the moment, completely without any anger? How can we describe it? This is a key question in finding a pathway to happiness. We will address it in the next chapter.

The Basis for Wisdom in Everyday Life

Let bewilderment, anxiety, anger
Wanting, shame, guilt and sorrow pass.
Bring your mind back to the present. (H 99)

When does anger arise? It does so when there is opposition within us to something happening. Any actual change, any perceived change, or merely the hint of a threat of any unwanted change may bring it on.

Anger is closely related to the emotional state of not-wanting. Whenever we do not want something to happen or wish to avoid anything changing, we are emotionally defensive. This is anger – and this emotional defensiveness is associated with angry intention, with a readiness for angry thoughts and angry impulses, thus for angry words and angry actions.

Attachment is preceded by want, by some form of desire. It provides the pre-condition for resistance and anger. Whenever we have an attachment, we naturally want to hold on to the object of that attachment, to counter any threat to it, to prevent change or loss in connection with it. We might say the opposite of anger then is a sense of acceptance.

To accept a change is the converse of resisting one. For the sake of equanimity – and thus happiness – it is better either to accommodate change, or accommodate oneself to it, which amounts to much the same thing. Even better, where possible, is to embrace change warmly, perhaps even tenderly and with kindness.

Here then is another useful pointer towards the opposite of anger. 'I feel no anger about what is happening' is equivalent to 'I feel okay about it', 'I feel happy about it', 'I accept it', 'I go along with it' or, 'I support it'. What is the pain-free emotion being referred to here? We have to call it something. Perhaps we should simply choose, according to circumstances: 'acceptance', 'kindness', 'tenderness' or 'warmth'.

As far as the basic, rudimentary emotions are concerned, when anger is absent, it is perhaps difficult to differentiate more closely than to think, 'I am happy and calm'. With experience perhaps we can also learn to discriminate further by adding, 'I am feeling gentle, affectionate, kind'. It has to do with us feeling emotionally soft and giving rather than hard and unyielding, with being comfortably warm rather than either burning hot or icy cold.

Reflecting on Anger – 1.

Walk about or sit down and try to work yourself up into a temper.

Think about something that might – or regularly does – upset you. Feel the irritation, the anger. Experience it to the full, but at the same time avoid being tempted to act on it. Do not waste the energy. Do not curse. Do not lash out with words or hit out with your fists. Clench them and unclench them a few times if you must, but pay attention to your breath. Watch it grow faster and maybe deeper. Notice too how your pulse may quicken. This is your body getting ready to fight. Observe it. Watch the breath again.

With your mind focused on your breathing, and no longer on whatever upsets you, watch your mind and your body eventually calm down. Take as long over this as necessary. Keep breathing. Recite your preferred phrase, your mind-protector, several times. Use your visual imagination if you like. Picture a tranquil scene, a riverbank or a beautiful lagoon on a sunny day, perhaps. In time, bring your mind gently back to the present.

When you are feeling calmer again, think in as detached a way as you can about the cause or focus of your anger. Think about what it could have been that you were resisting – some kind of a change, something new to you, a new idea or some other kind of challenge to something you cherish, something you would not wish to be separated from, to have harmed or be taken away. Find out like this how deeply you care about things, about ideas and, of course, about people.

Remember this exercise when you become angry in everyday life. Take a little time out, observe and reflect. This can be very useful. It helps us to stay in control, and to discover what are our true priorities and values.

It is good to spend a lot of time thinking about things like this, and about the emotions concerned. Here is a warning, though. Try always to avoid speaking or acting from anger. You will only risk making things worse. If you think you will feel better, think deeply about it again. How long will it be before you are irritated like this next time? How much will your demonstration of anger be upsetting to others, those you meant to hurt and those you did not? Try as often as possible to act out of kindness, and with a clear mind. If you do, you will soon make things start to feel better again.

Anger arises from desire and want, from attachment. It is associated with not-wanting, aversion, the precursor of dislike, of hatred, therefore of hostility, aggression, violence and destruction.

Moreover, anger is associated with confusion, with an unclear mind. It is hard to think straight when you are angry. It is hard for us to consider and weigh up the consequences of our words and actions. It is too easy through anger to disregard them. In consequence, everyone pays.

Acceptance and kindness, gentleness, on the other hand, leading to calm as they do, serve to promote clarity of mind. Words and actions that arise out of such clarity are more likely to be helpful to all involved in the situation, to be constructive. This is the basis for wisdom in everyday life.

Seeing things clearly from all angles and doing what is best for everyone when changes, harm and losses threaten – this is the way of wisdom, the way of enlightenment and compassion. Admittedly this is often easier for us to say than to achieve.

Reflecting on Anger – 2.

Sit quietly again or go for a walk. Let your mind settle. After a while, bring to mind a recent occasion when you found yourself growing angry. Spend some time reflecting on the situation. There are valuable lessons to be learned.

It may help as you reflect to ask yourself certain questions. 'How was I feeling earlier in the day or shortly before becoming angry?' 'What was in the background?' 'Was I already feeling somewhat under threat?' 'Was I feeling rushed, in a hurry, impatient?'

Now it may help you to examine the trigger factors. Ask yourself, 'What made me angry then?' 'What sparked it off?' 'What actually happened?' 'Who was involved, someone close or a stranger?' 'What were my expectations of that person (or those people)?' 'Were those expectations realistic and justified, or was I (with hindsight) expecting a little too much?' 'Was I putting my needs and wishes before those of others?' 'Who was I angry with at the time – no-one at all, or someone else?' 'How angry was I with myself at the time?' 'How angry am I still – with the others involved as well as with myself?'

Finally, it may help to think about what happened to your emotions after the angry episode. You can use questions like, 'Have I begun to accept what took place?' 'Are my feelings beginning to soften?' 'When and how did this occur?' 'Was there a change in my thinking which helped to bring about acceptance and the lessening of my anger?' 'As my anger softened, what other awkward or even painful feelings took its place?' 'Did I feel any doubt or confusion?' 'Did I feel any guilt or shame as a result of acknowledging (at least some) responsibility for the incident?' 'Do I feel any shame about having got angry, and any guilt about things I did and said – or things I failed to do and say?'

When you have had enough of this questioning, relax. Bring your mind back to your surroundings, to the present moment. Congratulate yourself. These exercises are tough. It does not matter if you do not think you have been doing them properly or getting anything from them except more bad feeling. They do become easier with practice and experience. You can try this one again later. Have confidence. Have courage. You are learning. It takes effort, and time.

Now, please continue your life.

This can be a very beneficial exercise, all the more worthwhile if we can be ruthlessly honest with ourselves while carrying it out. It is an example of an important method of achieving personal growth, of gaining maturity. Through this particular kind of contemplative analysis, whereby one examines by not only thinking about but also experiencing emotions at the same time, we gradually gain mastery over them.

Being able to return to the still-point in the present moment, in the here and now, is the key. When we learn to be adept at this, there is little to lose by facing our anger and fears. There is really so much to gain.

Anger, Attachment and Letting Go

17

There is no world outside the mind.
We experience the world in our minds. (H 34)

How do we get from anger to happiness?

It is a matter of trusting a natural process. Just as nature provides for the healing of lacerations and fractures, so it does too for our emotional wounds. Anger is a response to the threat of either harm to, or loss of, something precious. It seems wrong to say that the path to resolution is surrender, letting go, giving up – but it is.

It can be helpful for us to recognise that it is the anger that must be given up, and not the precious object – at least not necessarily.

The mature way to deal with all painful emotions is threefold: first to acknowledge and experience them fully, then to take responsibility for them, finally to let them go, to let them pass by and watch them be naturally transformed into their polar opposite. This is why learning to sit quietly, paying attention to the emotions, thoughts, sense perceptions and impulses that disturb the mind can be so helpful.

What happens is that you learn to be patient with your emotions, to identify and observe them as they arise and as they diminish. As you grow calmer, the thoughts and feelings naturally separate out from one another. The Latin word for this process is 'lysis'. Lysis of the emotions is linked with, and complementary to, catharsis. (See Chapter 12.) As the process of lysis goes forward, on the one side are the emotions, and on the other are the thoughts they are linked to. They become distinguishable, and now you can deal in a more detached and effective way with the situation than if you were to let anger, doubt, fear or bewilderment rule your thoughts, actions and words.

The best emotional state to think clearly in, to speak and act from, is one of calm and joyful equanimity. This is worth bearing in mind, even if it is not always easy.

Emotional Responsibility – Revisiting the Rogers Family.

Sit quietly, alone and in comfort. Relax. Close your eyes if you wish.

Now bring to mind the story of the Rogers family. You may like to read through Chapter 13 again. Reflect on how the anger and misunderstanding within the family gave rise to distress and conflict that could not at first be resolved. Who seemed to be taking responsibility for their own emotions, thoughts and actions when they went to see the therapist? Who in the family seemed to be blaming someone else – Stephen – for most of the problems? What needed to happen before resolution could occur?

Now, can you think of any comparable situations in your own life, from the past or still current? If so, reflect on one of these for a while. Try to allow yourself to feel the emotions, painful though they may be. Allow yourself to suffer these experiences. Try to have confidence that they will pass – also that you will be enriched. Be as honest with yourself as you can.

Now consider this. How often do you habitually think of others as responsible for your feelings, good or bad? How hard would it be for you, little by little perhaps, to begin taking more emotional responsibility for yourself? It may help to ask yourself, 'What am I protecting myself from?' 'What do I really fear?' Also, 'What is the worst that could happen if I did face what I fear?'

Remember to keep your emotions in balance as you give this exercise a try. Stop when you need or want to and focus once more on your breath or your mantra. Wait until you feel calm and contented again before going on with your life. Also, please return to this exercise whenever you wish.

In the Rogers family, young Lucy had a life-threatening illness, but it was her brother Stephen's irritable mood and behaviour that was particularly upsetting Carol, David and Chrissie. Their anxiety found a focus outside themselves in Stephen. He had effectively drawn their emotional fire, so to speak. They naturally became impatient and at times frankly angry with him in return.

When the therapist pointed out to them that they were not facing the real possibility that Lucy might have died and might still perish from her diabetes, there was a silent acknowledgement in all members of the family. The truth about the possible loss that threatened could not be denied or avoided any more. It had to be faced and accepted by all, and this led to a change in the emotional climate within the family. Each person, thinking about his or her own sense of loss, started to become sad rather than anxious or angry.

In the light of this new insight, it was no longer appropriate to feel angry with Stephen. He could not be accused of causing Lucy's illness in the first place, and his extreme sadness ensured too that he could rejoin the family, being emotionally united with the others once more in the sharing of this deep sorrow.

If, by chance, you were shocked or surprised at the Rogers' story, and unsure of its eventual happy outcome, please be confident that the sadness in this family passed, and that they were able to make a new start together, realistically facing a problem that was now uniting them emotionally, rather than splitting them apart. A good sign of this satisfactory development was Lucy's change of attitude towards wanting to take increasing responsibility for the treatment of her own illness.

The essential point for us to grasp is that, even when facing the genuine threatened loss of Lucy's life, nothing really bad actually happened. It only felt that way for a time. Lucy's life was not lost. In fact, through her change of attitude, it was somehow regained. The threat, although still there, had been made to retreat. Thus it was not the object of affection, Lucy, that the family lost and had to surrender (although it felt like it). It was their anxiety and anger that they gave up, initially in favour of sadness, and then in favour of joy.

Reflections on Attachment and Loss.

Sit quietly, alone and in comfort, and think this through once more. Identify something or someone you are strongly attached to, some idea, some object, some activity or someone precious. If you like, perhaps try to pick one example from each category.

Now, reflect on this attachment. What does it mean to you? How would your emotions be affected if this valued thing were in some way threatened? An activity, such as a sport you enjoy, might be threatened by either injury or some interruption, for example. How would you feel if your dearest pet were wounded or taken away? How would your emotions be affected if the threat were of permanent loss rather than temporary harm, prevention or separation? What would you think? What might you say – to yourself, to anyone responsible for the threat or loss of something precious? What might you say to God if someone you loved were badly hurt or died tragically young? In the face of monumental loss, do you know what you might do?

Now, keeping these questions in mind, think about them according to three timescales – as if at the point of threat, over the following hours and days, and from some time in the future, perhaps years. Draw on both your experiences of life and your imagination.

How deep, how strong, how powerful have you discovered your attachment to valued ideas, items, activities or persons to be? Now consider if anything about these objects of your attachment has changed in the last few minutes while you have been doing this exercise. Whatever thoughts, feelings and impulses you have been having, however powerful they are, surprising though it may seem, little or nothing will have actually changed. Despite the magical notion that our very thoughts can alter reality, from a more objective point of view, everything in the world will be much the same. It is worth spending time reflecting on this.

When you are ready, recall yourself to the present moment. Come back now to just sitting. If you have been troubled or excited by your thoughts and feelings, wait until you feel at peace again once more. If you like, focus your mind once more on your breath or your mantra. When you are calm, get up and return to your life.

Degrees of attachment are important. The same object, for example, can excite us one day and bore us the next. Attachment may turn into indifference overnight. Boredom and indifference can also quickly become dislike, aversion. Aversion and anger are obviously linked.

In this chapter, we have touched on the idea that attachment to something can be reduced or relinquished entirely, without the object of that attachment actually being altered or lost. This is important to grasp, because unhappiness depends on attachments, and happiness therefore depends on giving them up. However, giving up attachment to things does not necessarily mean giving up the things themselves. Rather, it is about a change of attitude. Many of us have difficulty understanding this point, which we will be addressing again later on.

The Origin of Suffering 18

Has it occurred to you
That a person can be happy,
Even in the face of death itself? (H 145)

If you reach a point of feeling fully prepared for any threat to any-thing and everything you are attached to, you will be a happier per-son. If you are attuned in acceptant readiness for loss, you will always be easier in your mind. When they come, threats and losses, as they must, you will be able to face them both with calm equanimity. So, if you wish, if you choose, if you take the opportunity, it is firstly an idea you have to come to terms with, the idea of loss, before the real loss of the actual thing itself.

This distinction between the attachment and the thing itself is signifi-cant. In the well-known biblical quotation it is 'the love of money' – attachment to it, the passion, the desire for it, the craving, the wish both to gain it and hold on to it – that 'is the root of all evil'.[9] It is not the money itself.

This is a subtle but important point. It means that at every moment we can prepare ourselves for losses and threats.

We can prepare for threat and loss by looking around more attentively, by taking stock. We can do so by making ourselves more aware of all that, perhaps unconsciously, we have been valuing and taking for grant-ed. Doing this can be painful at first. If we were blind, for example, how would it be? If we were to lose our hearing, our senses of smell, taste

[9] 1 Timothy 6 v 10.

and touch, if we were no longer able to write or to read: if any or all of these were the case, how would it be? How would each of us feel?

It can be painful to ask ourselves soul-searching questions like these, but it can also bring us to a kind of renewal, giving us each new energy, new enthusiasm, a new lease of life.

Thinking about Losing Something We Usually Take for Granted.

Go, if you can, into a garden or to some other beautiful place. Alternatively, choose some beautiful object – a single flower perhaps – beautiful in itself, rather than as any kind of a symbol of wealth or success. Sit or stand somewhere quietly. Close your eyes. Let your thoughts and feelings grow calm.

Now, remaining still, open your eyes, open your ears, open your nostrils and take it all in. Experience and appreciate the sights, sounds and smells in that place where you are at this very present moment.

After a minute or so, close your eyes once again. Imagine they were fixed and could not be re-opened. (It is harder to switch off hearing and the sense of smell, but perhaps you can imagine this too.) Reflect upon what, if you happened to be blind, deaf and with no sense of smell, you would be asked to give up in terms of the scene upon which you were focusing just now. Give free rein to your emotions. Take note of what you feel. Is there within you any sensation of loss? If so, for the next few moments, pay attention to that.

Eventually, and very consciously, open your eyes once again. How does it feel to get your eyesight back? (How does it feel to be able to hear again and to smell?) Is there relief and renewal? Is there a greater sense of beauty and the value of beauty?

Finally, take a breath and walk away from the beautiful scene. Turn your head for a final look before you leave if you wish. Now, please, return once more to your life.

We can all take comfort in noting that whatever happens, beauty will always be there somewhere. So, even if we should happen to find ourselves blind one day, however badly we feel, everything is not utterly lost. In the first place, we will have memory to conjure up the sights and sounds. We may feel grateful about this. We will know that there is beauty in the world, whether we have immediate access to it or not. This is reassuring when beauty, and the feelings of joy, peace and contentment which accompany it, seem lost or far away. We have the blessings of our imagination to bring some of it back. Obviously, the more each of us has encountered beauty – and taken proper note of it – the easier for us this will be.

It must be admitted, however, that there are circumstances in which fear and resistance grow strong.

*

As humans, our tendency is to cling powerfully, tenaciously to life. Injury, illness and ageing all seem to threaten life, and are often among our strongest aversions. The idea of death itself, bringing pain and oblivion, would seem to be the worst we could face.

Again it is useful for us to note that it is the *idea* of something that seems to be at the root of the problem, not the thing itself – whether it be injury, illness, ageing or death. More subtly, the idea of oblivion, of non-existence, of the world going on without us, is as much a threat to our personal integrity – to that which we are to ourselves – as is death. This threat is quite common, for example whenever we feel ignored by somebody significant, or left out of a situation where we feel we belong.

So, looking again at these major threats of injury, illness, ageing, death and oblivion, let us consider how they might be avoidable. Then let us consider some of the ways people try and deal with them.

It has been said that the true origin, the primary cause of suffering is birth. This seems to mean that, as soon as we have a body, the risks of injury, illness, ageing and death exist. They cannot be avoided. Once we have a mind and are conscious, we learn about the ways of things and perhaps encounter injury, illness, ageing and death as they affect others. We will then be subject not only to the threat of these things, but also susceptible even to the idea of them.

Here, perhaps, in our desire to continue living and to avoid all possible threats, are the true origins of anxiety and the birth of fear. This wish to avoid threat is a form of desire that precedes anxiety and specific fears. It also precedes angry resistance to threatening change, and sorrow and grief in the face of actual loss.

Illness, Injury, Ageing and Death.

Sit quietly and alone. Spend a few minutes quietening down, allowing your thoughts and emotions to settle, your mind to clear. Watch your breath or use your reminder-phrase, your mantra, if you wish.

Now, when you are calm and alert, think in turn about each of these possible threats – injury, illness, ageing and death. What do they signify for you in regard to yourself? What do they signify when you think about someone else, perhaps a parent, a child or your beloved? What emotions arise as you consider these matters? Observe the feelings that arise. Experience them and watch them develop, changing in intensity and in nature.

Now come back to the present. Allow your thoughts and feelings to settle. When you are calm again, ask yourself how you normally cope day by day with the idea of these threats – injury, illness, ageing, death and oblivion. Do they preoccupy you, do you sometimes think about them, or do you ignore them? Are you able to put them completely out of your mind? What general approach do you use, and what kind of strategies are you aware of others using to deal with them? Could some of these strategies be more successful than others? How much, for instance, do people tend to deny these threats? How many people do you know who seem to think and behave as if they were genuinely invulnerable, as if they were going to live healthily and without accident forever? In answering these questions, be as truthful with yourself as you can.

Now relax once more. Focus your mind on the here and now. Ask yourself, 'What threat of injury or illness am I realistically under at this immediate moment? What is the likely risk as I sit here of sudden death?' We age, of course, at the exact rate of one minute per minute, one hour every hour. How does it feel when you reflect on the thought that there is nothing you – or anyone – can do about that?

Make sure you are fully focused in the present, calm and happy again, before you return to your life.

The strategies we use to deal with the inevitable threats of injury, illness, ageing and death, if they involve any measure of denial, can be effective in the short term, but usually ultimately collapse. This eventual failure tends to bring more intense and lasting suffering, misery, even despair than would be the case if by due preparation we each allowed our self a realistic appraisal of genuine risk, and had accepted the emotional consequences earlier.

To deal with the risk of mishap or injury, one strategy is to turn it on its head, to indulge deliberately in activities that are dangerous. Many outdoor and sporting activities, such as skiing, parachuting and mountaineering, cater for this approach, but under conditions of relative and intelligent safety. The same pastimes can also be practised less safely, involving behaviour which is more potentially destructive.

Danger itself seems to be addictive. There is also a perverse satisfaction in risky habits known to lead to injuries and fatalities, like the use of tobacco, the abuse of alcohol and other dangerous drugs, or in driving too fast. This type of strategy involves gambling sometimes with the lives and safety of others.

Gambling involves taking risks and trying 'to beat the odds'. But the odds on loss, harm, injury or illness at some point in our lives, from birth onwards, are almost unavoidably high. It seems best for us not to feel angry and aggrieved, or to blame bad luck when things go wrong, but to be genuinely emotionally prepared. This is a form of emotional maturity that will benefit not only us, but also everyone else.

Ageing and death are usually late-life occurrences, but they are even more certain than injury and illness. Of course early death prevents ageing, but let us consider how people seek to deny and avoid the idea of both.

One strategy is to promote a culture of youth and fitness, health and beauty. This can be taken beyond normal precautions considered appropriate and sensible. In one kind of denial we take risks by avoiding good advice, or we might have a self-defeating tendency to overdo it, or we rely on appearance rather than true inner health and harmony.

This culture is allied closely with a kind of devotion to celebrity, to sexual attractiveness, to skin-deep 'charisma', to power, wealth and success. In the following chapters we will explore whether these relatively prevalent values truly point towards happiness. By failing to deal truthfully with the genuine threats of injury, illness, ageing, death and oblivion faced by everyone who has ever been born, these strategies impede and divert energy away from full resolution of natural anxieties and fears.

There are less damaging, more mature strategies to use in the face of these major challenges – humour, for example. Do you know the joke about the three people in an airplane that is about to crash, in which there are only two parachutes? Do you know one in which someone arrives at Heaven's Gate, seeking admission?

Jokes about death and dying are legion, and can allay our anxiety about the subject for a brief time. There is, however, a yet more mature way to proceed: to face reality, without denial, moment by moment, firmly anchored in the present. This way we can keep our equanimity. We can stay clear-minded, in touch with stillness and joy. In the face of ageing, illness, injury, death and oblivion, we may even find ourselves smiling.

Happiness – Step by Step 19

Teach yourself how to be silent,
Learn how to discover that this happy moment
Is the eternal present. (H 153, 154)

Once you taste the water at the bottom of the well, the water within, the water of such intense joy and calm, of such bliss, your heart will truly sing. It will remember the song it only *seems* to have forgotten. In comparison, all the pleasures of the world will seem dull. Although you may doubt now that this is possible, earthly pleasures will feel like what they really are – another subtle form of suffering.

Any pleasure you can think of, however appealing, is impermanent. Even if such things were to last, our senses inevitably pall after a time. We grow weary of even the most pleasant things. In contrast, true happiness and tranquillity do not depend on worldly conditions, and are not affected by the passage of time. These emotional states are there for us to access through stillness of mind at any moment. Once accessed, their quality is timeless. So, by keeping our minds focused constantly in the stillness of the present, the sensation we experience is like that of entering eternity. This is the condition achieved by the emotionally mature mind, one devoid of the self-seeking ego.

*

'Ego' is a much-used and often misunderstood word. In Latin it simply means 'I'. The essential characteristic of this 'I', this 'ego', which brings about emotional pain, is its inseparability from desire, from attachment, from wanting. This is because, first and foremost, it is attached to itself. It is attached to itself like a limpet.

A second characteristic of the ego is for it to identify with – and stick almost equally firmly to – all manner of things: for example to people, possessions, results, ideas and beliefs. Each of us has an ego-self that can hold on incredibly tightly, and attachments like this can soon come to feel more like burdens than pleasures.

It is important to understand that the secret is not necessarily for us to give up the objects of attachment, but to give up attachment itself. This means letting go. It means allowing the emotional process to run its natural course, so that the painful aspect of each emotion is converted to its pain-free version. Want becomes contentment, bewilderment develops into clarity, doubt gives way to certainty, shame and guilt to self-worth and innocence. Anxiety turns into calm, anger into gentle acceptance and sorrow becomes joy. Sitting quietly with our feelings, being patient with them, however powerful and deeply felt, permits this happy and natural metamorphosis.

Usually one unpleasant emotion from the set listed in Chapter 15 gives rise to another, like a run through the musical scale. Sometimes they all thunder at once in a single cacophony. If they are too intense for us, too painful, nature will ensure a catharsis, a release of emotional energy. Often this is brought about through tears, or by expressing our feelings as physical symptoms. Then we need to pay attention to what our bodies are trying to tell us, and work out the significance of these messages in terms of our attachments.

Oblivion – Feeling Ignored.

Sit quietly and alone once more. If you wish, first make yourself a hot drink. Make yourself comfortable. Hold the cup. Feel the warmth. Taste the taste.

Now, try and recall a recent occasion when you felt out of place, slighted or ignored. Perhaps you spoke to somebody and they seemed not to hear you, turning away. You wanted them to take notice. How did you feel at the time? Can you re-create the feelings now in your imagination? Were you anxious before you approached the person? Were you bewildered at first when your approach was ignored? Did you feel momentary doubt, followed quickly by shame or guilt, as if to say to yourself, 'Is this really happening? Have I gone about this the wrong way?' Perhaps you began to feel a measure of irritation or anger, directed towards either yourself or the other person. Finally, as you began to accept the failure of your approach on this occasion, did you feel, however fleeting, a moment of sadness? How long did it take to calm down? When your mind was clear (and happier) once more, did you think of a better strategy for gaining the attention of the person you wanted to take notice of you? If not, could you do so right now?

Take as long as you like over this exercise (but remember to enjoy your hot drink!). When you are ready, relax and return to your life.

By paying attention to our feelings, working towards mastering them rather than letting them dominate us, we will gradually become more skilful at distinguishing them in our minds. We can watch and witness our emotions separate out, not only from each other but also from the attachments to which we are still holding on.

The process of deconstruction, of 'lysis', of the separation of everyday emotions into their component thoughts, words, impulses, actions and the basic emotions involved, complements that of catharsis. Our task is to do our best to let it happen unhindered.

This task requires practice to develop the skill of combining alertness with relaxation. In the example from the exercise above, wanting to be noticed and perhaps given credit for something, we would naturally be seeking to preserve self-esteem. What the ego wants is not always a sense of importance but simply one of existence.

'Ego' translates from Latin not only as, 'I', but also as, 'I am'. This sense of existence, of being, is fairly essential in everyday life, but we can do without it. For example, we give it up whenever we go to sleep. Furthermore, selflessness – putting self more or less consciously aside for the benefit of other people – is a human ideal for many. Emotional maturity and the capacity for selflessness have a tendency to go together.

The rewards of being able to observe our thoughts and emotions in this way make it a priceless skill worth acquiring, and not least because the rewards are lasting. The benefits are permanent.

The benefits to us are permanent because every threat thoroughly weathered and every loss utterly sustained will invoke and exercise our entire emotional system. The process has to go to completion. The whole range or spectrum of bad feelings must somehow come into play and be experienced. Then, through a combination of catharsis and lysis – the release of emotions and release of the ego-self from its attachments – a new, more stable and happier equilibrium will be reached. We will be able to experience and tolerate greater intensities of emotional experience, both happy and sad, our own and other people's, with increased equanimity.

This means that not only are the specific incidents resolved successfully and satisfactorily, but also the emotional system becomes more resilient, better able to deal in the future with losses and threats. The balance is shifted permanently towards the happy side of the emotional equation, away from the painful side. Depending upon the magnitude and nature of the losses faced successfully, this improvement may sometimes only be small, but it will always be irreversible. This also means that each step can be built upon. Gains of this nature accumulate. Emotional maturity is achieved incrementally, stage by stage.

Do We Gain from our Losses?

Go for a walk, or sit quietly at home. Look around you. Open your senses. Look, listen, touch, smell. Breathe in and out consciously. Try a smile.

Now, when you are feeling relaxed and happy enough, think about a recent loss or some other difficult situation you have encountered. Ask yourself, 'How well did I cope with that?' 'Did

I cope poorly, satisfactorily or really well?' What does this mean in terms of how you felt, what you said (or did not say) and what you did (or did not do)?

Now ask yourself, 'If this had happened to me earlier in my life – say three to five years ago – would I have coped as well?' Next ask yourself, 'What has made the difference?' Did an earlier emotionally painful situation teach you something that has been helpful this time? Do painful emotions now seem somehow easier to face?

After thinking about this for a while, bring your mind back to the present, to where you are. Use your breath or your mantra as a focus if necessary. Are you aware of having been frowning? Why not try a smile once more?

Here are two almost contradictory statements. A sensation of eternal bliss may be accessed at any time by a still and tranquil mind, free of desire, free of grasping. The path towards happiness in everyday life is a steady and lengthy one, continuous, with few obvious and reliable short cuts.

There is an element of mystery here, and also the potential for confusion. In trying to understand the point, it is helpful for us to reflect on the nature of emotional experience in everyday life. In doing so, we need to recognise the many different temperaments people may have. We also need to note our changing moods, lasting hours or days, as well as the fact that emotions can fluctuate minute by minute, in response to a multitude of factors.

Our everyday emotions are mercurial. They change rapidly in nature and intensity. They are affected by degrees of fatigue or alertness, and they alter so rapidly that often they become blurred. They confuse us by switching from comfortable to uncomfortable, from pleasant to unpleasant, from pain-free to painful, from okay to awry, from happy to unhappy, instant by instant. Ambivalence is our natural state. It will help us now, in the following chapters, to look again more closely at the nature of attachment, and to do so we will also explore processes leading to resolution of the emotional pain that accompanies loss.

Displaced Feelings – Mandy's Story

Come back from anger and fear to your true home.
Return to the here and now!
Simply breathe . . . Simply be,
And be happy. (H 158)

At first it may sound odd, but at times some people seem to prefer anger to other emotions, even the pleasant ones. This may be because anger makes us feel powerful, ready to act. So it is sometimes easier for us to remain angry than to let what may seem like weakness creep in. But anger often conceals sadness and fear. If anger persists, the natural process of emotional resolution towards happiness is prevented, and this means that anger cannot prevail without ultimately resulting in more pain and destruction than would otherwise have occurred. In any case, anger cannot be sustained forever. It must eventually give way.

Here is another true story. Some years ago, a psychiatrist was invited to visit the children's wards of a specialist hospital. Many of the children had heart disease, and they came here to have operations. Sometimes the children were only a few hours or days old. Often life-saving surgery had to be followed up later by further procedures, as the children – and their hearts – grew in size.

Obviously, you cannot operate on the human heart without taking a risk, and most of these baby hearts were malformed and performing poorly, adding to the danger. Inevitably in some cases surgery was unsuccessful and the child could not be saved. Worse perhaps, in some cases children survived, but with their health severely impaired. For example, their heart may have stopped beating effectively for a time, resulting in damage to the brain. Alternatively, their heart simply did not beat sufficiently strongly to maintain a circulation viable enough for the child to lead any kind of active life.

When a child came into this hospital, often far away from the family home, rather spare accommodation was also provided for a relative. It was usually the child's mother who stayed. The psychiatrist was told that some of these mothers were difficult for doctors and nurses to deal with. He was asked for advice.

The psychiatrist returned to the hospital regularly for an afternoon once a week over a period of more than two years. He spoke to many mothers and some fathers. He spoke to doctors (including surgeons), to nurses, social workers, physiotherapists and play therapists. He even spoke to some of the older children themselves. As a result of numerous conversations and interviews, he began to build up a picture of what seemed to be going on at the emotional level. On the surface, more or less everybody seemed frustrated or angry, and usually they were angry with someone. Also, there seemed to be rules about this anger. It arose in ways that made it hard to resolve.

For example, some mothers got angry with the nurses, who felt in response that they were doing their best and that the mothers' anger was unreasonable. It may be that these mothers were really angry with the doctors or surgeons about some of the decisions they were making, but they did not have the opportunity to express this – they did not see senior medical staff very often and did not want to seem antagonistic when they did. This is why some of their anger was displaced from the doctors to the nurses. Because it landed in the wrong place and felt unreasonable, it could not be resolved satisfactorily or conclusively. A mother's anger was often also based on anxiety about what was happening at home, and what she was going to have to tell her husband and her other children about the sick child's progress. A mother in this situation often felt alone and under-supported.

Anger also tended to be displaced across professional boundaries and between levels in the various hierarchies. Nurses found it easier to be angry with mothers who complained than with doctors and surgeons or with more senior nurses, but the anger towards medics and their superiors was there, even when it was not being shown.

For example, junior nurses were sometimes angry with the ward sister, either for not standing up to the doctors or for not coping better with angry mothers. Because it was not easy for some nurses to express their anger, it seemed easier for them to complain among themselves; and perhaps also to take it out, for example, on the physiotherapists, who might feel aggrieved in their turn. As a result of all this, there appeared to be no love lost between the various professional groups.

The psychiatrist found initially that people were keen to be interviewed alone about how they saw the problems in the surgical and intensive care wards. Individual cases were discussed in private. 'I don't think they should have operated on Mandy,' a nurse or a physio might say, for example. 'She was not well enough. When she went down for surgery, I was really afraid she might not make it. She had been here two weeks and we were gradually getting her better. I'm sure of it, even if the tests weren't improving. I think Mr Smith (the surgeon) should have waited a bit longer. If they had waited, Mandy might not have died. But her mother insisted. She thought Mandy was getting worse and the operation would save her.'

For the psychiatrist, taken into people's confidence in this privileged way, the essential problem seemed all too clear. It was not a question of who made what decision. It was simply that children do become ill and, despite everyone's best efforts, some of them fail to survive.

Mandy's Story – the Different Perspectives.

Sit quietly, alone and in comfort. Be prepared to confront some painful feelings.

Think about Mandy and the scenario described. Remember, the physiotherapist or the nurse is angry. Ask yourself what feelings you think her (or his) anger might be concealing. Ask yourself how you might be feeling in a similar situation. To what other feelings does a sense of helplessness give rise?

Now think about these events from the point of view of Mr Smith, the surgeon. Would or should emotions play a part in his decision-making in your opinion? Where does compassion fit in?

Now think about Mandy's mother. Imagine that she has a husband and other young children at home. What might she be thinking as the surgeon tries to explain why he thinks it is better to operate on Mandy than to wait any longer? What emotions might she be feeling at various stages: as the decision is made, as Mandy is taken to the operating theatre, as she is returned to the ward after unsuccessful surgery and as she dies later on in the day? Imagine this really is you, and someone you love dearly has been operated on today and has died. If you feel angry or sad, allow these feelings to develop. Release them. Pay attention to them. Observe and experience them. Respect them. Let them teach you. Name them, if you can. Describe them to yourself. Ask yourself, 'How does this feel?'

If you are feeling bad, ask yourself if you are also feeling bad about that. Pay attention not only to your feelings, but also to your feelings about your feelings. Learn from the experience. Watch and feel yourself grow.

Now pause, and take comfort from the observation that you have been reacting to an idea rather than an actual loss.

Finally, when you are ready, take a breath. Look around. Bring your mind back to the present moment. Let calm and happiness gradually return.

Having reacted with anger, sadness or other feelings to this true story about Mandy, we are likely to appreciate our own loved ones a little more, to be more aware of what they mean to us. Hopefully, we will be a little less fearful – perhaps also a little less angry – whenever their health and safety are threatened again.

Reading this account, many will think simply how sad is the story of Mandy, failing to survive an operation on her heart that was intended to restore her to an active and near-normal life. It may be hard to appreciate that at the time there was the most terrific desire on everyone's part for her to survive and do well, as well as an immense anxiety that she might not. During her two weeks on the ward before her operation, professional people got to know and grow fond of her. Working hard on her behalf strengthened this natural affection and attachment to her. But no-one was able to help Mandy once the decision to go ahead with surgery had been made and she was taken to theatre.

Doubt reigned in several minds about the wisdom of this decision. Some even felt a little shame at not having tried even harder for Mandy (though everyone was part of a team that had been doing its experienced best). Some may also have felt guilt at not asserting more effectively their views about delaying the operation. What the psychiatrist noted every time, in a number of cases like this one, was intense frustration and anger. What he did not yet see, what no-one showed him openly, was sorrow. But, of course, all the time, it was there.

Sharing Suffering and Discovering Compassion

Anger, desire, bewilderment,
Doubt, guilt and shame
Split and splinter the mind.
But sorrow may restore happiness.
Sorrow sometimes brings healing. (B 25)

In the Children's Hospital, the psychiatrist eventually decided that it might help if people came together regularly to share their thoughts and feelings about events taking place in the surgical unit. He offered to run a support group for the nurses. It seemed best to offer this opportunity to just one professional group to begin with, and the nurses made up the biggest group. They were keen to accept on condition that it did not keep them away too long from their patients. Those who attended group meetings deserve considerable thanks and credit for showing great courage. They were all candid in sharing their thoughts, and revealing with regard to their feelings.

The meetings usually began with a short period of silence. This allowed everybody to settle down and bring their concentration to bear on what they were doing now and not on what they had just been working on or what they had to do later. If there were strong feelings at play, these were usually harder to put aside, and some of the group meetings had to start with people acknowledging and unpicking these. If there were no obvious starting place, the psychiatrist would usually ask group members to recount recent success stories first. This was to help participants remind themselves and each other of the many favourable results of their work. It seemed important to acknowledge and enjoy the successes and the happy times.

Of course a good outcome also meant a child going home, and that was a loss – albeit a happy one – to be faced. In these groups, male as well as female nurses were able to acknowledge just how attached to and fond of their patients they tended to become.

As well as good news, more or less every week there would also be a story like Mandy's. 'What happened? 'Tell me the facts,' the psychiatrist would often say, 'And then we'll take a look at the feelings.'

Usually one of the more experienced nurses gave a brief, accurate and matter-of-fact account of some recent tragedy. Then those with strong feelings, especially those who were angry, took their turn. Others joined in with their observations and comments, perhaps offering an opinion about, for example, whether surgery had been mistimed. Often, especially during the earlier meetings or when newcomers joined the group later on, it was left to the psychiatrist to raise the question of sorrow. 'Do any of you feel sad about what has occurred?'

he might ask, or, 'Do any of you ever cry?' It was really a question of giving people permission to admit it.

When the groups began, tears from professional staff on this unit were fairly taboo. It was an unwritten rule: no one was supposed to cry at work. Rather than being seen as a natural reaction, tears seemed to signify failure, so they were not tolerated. But, as the group meetings revealed, professionals very often felt sad and did indeed cry from time to time.

'I cry at home,' said one nurse. 'I cried on the bus yesterday,' said another. 'I go to the sluice room to cry,' said a third. More or less everybody cried somewhere sometime. They tried to suppress it and, when successful at doing so, often seemed to grow angry. They concealed their sorrow and therefore felt ashamed about it. They released it in secret, as they all admitted, and usually then began to feel better.

This is the benefit of catharsis. But sometimes when the nurses cried, they also began to get in touch with their anger. This then had to be acknowledged and dealt with somehow. Part of the important work of the group was for all to discover that both anger and sorrow were not only natural and ultimately irrepressible reactions to major loss, and that crying – catharsis – was helpful, but also that it was something to be proud of and in a way pleased about, rather than ashamed. It meant you really cared. If you care, if you have compassion, it hurts. The more you care, the more it will hurt. The hurting means that you care. And in the group, the nurses themselves said that you can't be a good nurse unless you care.

It Hurts to Care.

Sit quietly again.

Now, think of an occasion when you felt both angry and sad because you cared, because the compassion within drove you towards some kind of crisis, some kind of immovable obstruction. Try and recall this episode in your life as clearly and as completely as possible. Take your time. Being blocked, perhaps you felt mystified, baffled, confused and helpless. Fighting the inevitable made you angry. Accepting it made you feel sad. Did you ever, in your anger, blame someone who might have been equally helpless? Have you ever felt accused by someone who was upset and hurt in a similar way, by someone who seemed to need to put the blame somewhere else?

Try and answer these questions truthfully. Take as long over them as you wish. Reflect too on how these situations are part of everyday life. Reflect on how much you care, on how much others care, and on how good it is to care.

Now, return to the present. Watch your breath. If necessary, use your mantra, your mind-protector, to regain equilibrium.

Now, smile. You are more mature as a person if you recognise that every life involves the ever-present risks of illness, injury, ageing and death, and that you do inescapably care for everyone facing these.

So, give yourself a smile and imagine a pat on the back, because in your deepest heart you really do care about everyone's welfare. This is compassion. It is a marvellous thing.

Later, one of the visiting mothers told the psychiatrist that she disliked the nurses on the children's ward because they never seemed to feel sad or upset. It was worse, she said, because they seemed to discourage others from showing their tears when those people were feeling the need for a really good cry.

It hurts to care, but it is as natural as breathing. Somehow in the deep well of our minds, we seem to know about suffering. We know intuitively when others are suffering. This telepathy, this automatic, intuitive sharing in the emotions of others is immediate. It arises in the present moment, in the here and now, and is called 'empathy'. Happy feelings as well as painful ones are infectious. This is an important point. Other people's emotions affect us. The unhappy nurses did not tell the mothers not to cry. They showed their complex feelings more directly, communicating their discomfort and displeasure in a powerful way.

If we are holding back strong feelings, say of anger or sadness, it will be obvious to others who are sensitive. This is why it is good to be in touch with our own feelings, even when they are painful. If we do not acknowledge them, it is all the more difficult for us to tolerate the existence and expression of them in others. If someone in a group feels unable to express their own feelings of anger, fear or sadness, for example, everyone else has to hold back their feelings, otherwise it seems an uncontrollable torrent or avalanche of painful emotion might begin. Unfortunately, the longer and more successfully they are avoided, the more dangerous such emotions (or even the threat of them) will feel. This is natural because the greater the dam, so to speak, the more powerful, prolonged and intense will be the flood when it breaks.

This is perhaps how it feels sometimes. A bereaved person might say, 'I am afraid that if I start to cry, I shall never stop.' But no catharsis goes on forever. There may be prolonged distress, and repetitive cycles of several emotions of varying intensity, both unhappy (which initially predominate) and happy (which eventually prevail). This can last a long time, but finally the grieving process will resolve. Equanimity is restored eventually.

The process is shorter and less painful for those who are better prepared, whose attachments are light, who are therefore more mature emotionally. This is usually those people who have already suffered, men and women who have been through the full spectrum of emotional experience many times, who have faced loss and accepted it, and have not only survived the experience but have found greater resilience in life's inevitable ups and downs. These are good people to seek out as leaders and teachers.

A Remarkable Transformation

A Remarkable Transformation

22

Sorrow, crying, tears . . . resolution!
The mind starts healing itself. (B 27)

One afternoon in the group at the Children's Hospital, something remarkable happened. All the bad feeling melted away.

In preceding weeks group members had often mentioned Darren, a boy of nine who had had a series of heart operations, the first when he was only a few days old. As a result of surgery, he had suffered some brain damage. Darren was physically disabled and very dependent, and was barely able to communicate by the time he was six years old. Despite the surgery his heart, lungs and circulation remained very weak. Nurses feared his mother, not because she was angry, but she had spent so much time on the paediatric and intensive care wards she seemed to know their jobs better than they did. They were sometimes concerned that she might see them doing something wrong or, more likely, failing to do something important. Her presence kept them on their toes, and they had very mixed feelings about this.

None of the decisions regarding Darren's care had been easy. Although unable to speak, he seemed a placid and happy child, uncomplaining and rewarding to nurse. He had been on and off vital life support in the unit for so long that all the nurses knew him well, and he was of course very popular. Recently though his strength had seemed to be failing week by week. On the morning of the group meeting in question, Darren, too weak to survive, had finally died.

At the outset feeling within the group was high. Nine or ten nurses were present, a few more than usual, and most of them were angry. There was no silence at the beginning. The psychiatrist soon guessed what had happened. One or two participants challenged him to take sides with them in accusing the doctors and surgeons. 'They just gave up on him,' someone said in disgust. 'Surely they could have tried harder.' There was a heated discussion about various measures that might have kept Darren alive longer, some of which had worked in the past. Even his mother was criticised for being too calm in the face of the crisis. 'How could she just sit there and watch him die?' someone asked. 'I couldn't have. It was agony. I just wanted them to put him back on the ventilator. I felt so helpless standing by. Why wouldn't they let me do my job and try to save him?'

The arguments continued for several minutes. Almost everyone wanted his or her say. They seemed to be of similar mind, and in a similar angry mood. Eventually one nurse who had been silent until then, sitting at the back of the small, winter-darkened room, said quietly, 'Maybe what happened to Darren was for the best.' Of everyone there, this nurse, Debbie, had probably known Darren and his mother the longest. It was brave of her to speak up.

What happened next was a silence – a very long, deep and sad silence. Without a word, we all went down to the bottom of that deep well of suffering and really explored it in our minds. We stayed down there together in the dark for quite a while. Then, eventually and gradually, we all began to return.

After Debbie's brave comment, there was no way for anyone present to deny that the time had passed for preventing the loss they feared, Darren's death. It was now irrevocable. In a healthy mind, when avoidance and denial are no longer options, acceptance simply must follow eventually. In this case all anxieties, confusion, doubts, shame and guilt, wanting things to be other than they truly were or could be, all anger, had dissolved at that moment into the purity of sorrow. We all felt bad. We all felt sad. But then, strangely, in our togetherness, in our sharing of feelings, gradually we began to feel better.

It seemed as if we sat together in silence for a long time, but it was only three or four minutes. Then something remarkable happened. All the bad feeling began simply melting away, and we began somehow to be healed of our pain.

Not only did all the bad feeling melt away, but it was also slowly replaced by its opposite components. Acceptance, the beginning of serenity, displaced the anger. The purity of sorrow cleared our minds of all remaining questioning, confusion and doubt. Contentment began replacing desire and aversion, for clearly there was no point now in wishing Darren back to a disadvantaged life and to the inevitable prospect of death again. Wisdom began to assert itself and prevail with the thought that, like it or not, this is how things are and must be.

With none of the group members still wishing things otherwise, shame and guilt lost their strength. In time quiet reflection brought satisfaction over a good job performed with the best of intentions to everyone's best ability. Within each person there was a renewed sense of pride, esteem for oneself both as a person and a professional, and pride in a team of people with real feelings alongside their training, abilities and skills. This, of course, was very good for morale.

Just Sitting.

Sit quietly in a tranquil place. Establish yourself in a good upright posture. Close, or nearly close, your eyes. Centre yourself in the present moment. Watch your breath or use your mantra. Allow yourself twenty or thirty minutes for this. Decide beforehand which it is to be and set a watch or a timer.

There is no object to this exercise other than for you to practise letting your mind free to find its own level. If you do this once or twice a day on a regular basis, your emotional life will grow less turbulent. You will gradually feel happier and more in control. Like Darren's mother, you will eventually be able to face the ultimate of bereavements with equanimity, wisdom, compassion for others and poise.

When the time you have allotted is over, take a full breath and open your eyes. A moment or two later, give a gentle stretch and move your head from side to side a little. With the third or fourth breath you will be ready to rise and return to your life.

What happened in the group that day seems to show two things about human emotions. It reveals how much we have them in common, automatically to be communicated and shared in situations where people identify with each other. It also demonstrates how closely related each emotion in the basic scale or spectrum is to each of the others. When they are all expressed together or in turn, without interference or interruption, the process resolves spontaneously, with the release of emotional pain and the founding of a new equilibrium. As the unhappy feelings subside, they naturally develop into their happier versions. The whole emotional system is then reset a notch or two towards the happier side – to the benefit of all.

Not only those attending the group that day gained from what happened there. It was to become clear in succeeding weeks that a real sea-change had occurred within the surgical unit.

Firstly, future group meetings were happier and far less tense. There was much less denial of the possibility of medical and surgical failure than previously, and a greater acceptance of possible – even probable – losses from time to time. There was therefore much less anger and defensiveness, and a greater appreciation of the efforts and skills of others. People were able to pay each other compliments more frequently and freely, to the great benefit of staff-staff and staff-parent relations. The atmosphere began to improve instantly.

Feeling more confident, individuals also began to speak up more often with suggestions for improving ward routine and procedures. For instance, instead of seeing parents, especially mothers, as a problem and waiting for them to come and share their anxieties, the nurses set up a new system. The unit social worker usually got to know the parents early on as part of her job. The nurses now invited her to join them once a week at a special meeting which they called a 'psycho-social ward round'. The purpose of this was to share relevant and useful information, flagging up significant factors in the life of the child's family, planning interventions and support where possible and appropriate.

Practical as well as emotional issues could be addressed. For example, when they learned that she also had a dying father to look after at home, staff became more spontaneously considerate and understanding of a parent who at first did not seem interested enough to visit and stay very often. She had not wanted to bother anyone with this additional problem, but it had been weighing her down. This explained why she always seemed to be over-reacting to her child's plight, which – as both doctors and nurses had tried to explain, apparently unsuccessfully – was not too serious. They told her that he was likely to recover completely.

This mother's anxiety and doubt had been making staff feel uncomfortable and tacitly criticised. Insight into her extra burden now relieved these feelings. Calm, confidence and clarity were restored by this new information which had been obtained through the new procedure resulting from the group's transformative experience. Anxiety, uncertainty and confusion were now very much diminished.

Having the courage to face the pain of loss, reaching right down to the renewing water at the bottom of that deep wellspring of emotion, ensured that both wisdom and compassion could prevail. It seems likely that this is the only reliable way.

Every Ending is a New Beginning

When you survive a loss,
You will have learned something new
About yourself, about others,
About the world, about life! (B 32)

The atmosphere of the group meetings at the Children's Hospital changed in the weeks after Darren's death and his mother's departure from the intensive care ward. The emotional resolution that had occurred seems to have marked an ending and a new beginning. There were fewer attenders each week and people had less to say and less to complain about, although this changed again later when there was a new intake of nurses.

Debbie, who had spoken up bravely, soon decided to apply elsewhere for a promotion and was successful. She left to take up a new position at another hospital. She found that choosing to go, and putting that choice into practice, was relatively effortless. When she looked, she discovered at once that a suitable post had been advertised. As she felt no untoward anxiety, coming across as confident, capable and spontaneous at interview, it is no surprise that she was offered the job, which she then experienced no hesitation in accepting. This seemingly easy type of passage often follows natural endings.

Many nurses had left this unit before, after enduring much pressure and experiencing less satisfaction than they had hoped for. But these men and women tended to remain ambivalent about some aspects of their work, especially what seemed to them unnecessary losses and failures. Some appropriately took time off, or sought less stressful work, giving themselves the opportunity to reflect on their experiences and continue to make better sense of them. Some gave up nursing altogether. Debbie simply felt ready for more responsibility, and for the opportunity to supervise others. In herself, she felt more mature. She had reached a natural end-point. To stay on, she said, would have felt wrong. She was ready to take with her the seeds of wisdom and compassion she had gained.

Whether we are fully aware of it or not, this is often how we recognise at a deep level when something, some situation or relationship we are involved in, has come to a natural end. There is a deep-seated change within our emotional system, and there is also usually an obvious way to go forward. What happens is that we give up not our love for something or someone, but a degree of our attachment to that object, activity, idea or person. We will be looking more closely at this point later.

Completion.

Sit quietly, alone and in comfort. Make yourself a warm drink again if you wish. Enjoy the warmth. Enjoy the aroma. Enjoy the taste.

Now, when you are ready, turn to your memories and see if you can bring to mind one or more occasions when it seemed as if you had reached completion or closure, some kind of natural end point, similar to that reached by Debbie. Think of how it came about. Was there something that you accepted, which perhaps you had been resisting earlier? Think about the emotional changes. Was there an identifiable sequence? Was there a major release of emotion, a catharsis, or was the process quieter and more gradual? Did the catharsis occur first, and then later the dawning of acceptance, the dawning of wisdom? To what extent are you aware that a new beginning followed this ending? Did you find it easy to make the necessary decisions? Did you feel confident of your choices? Could what happened have occurred if you had not been through the earlier process, the emotional shake-up?

Spend as much time as you like reflecting on these matters. You may find that you want to talk about them with someone. If so, think for a moment now about the people you trust with your thoughts and feelings. Do you have someone you feel comfortable with, someone you can really confide in? Is there more than one person? If you were to meet other people in a group once a week to share your experiences, thoughts and feelings, who among your family, friends and acquaintances would you like to be there? Make a list, either on paper or in your mind. Who would you wish to avoid having as a fellow group member?

When you are ready, please return to your life.

The process of grieving, the emotional reaction to bereavement and loss that ideally ends with liberation, release and renewal, has to begin with attachment. If there were no attachment, there would be no prospect of loss. Attachment here means emotional attachment of the 'I', the ego, to something – indeed to anything. This is the investment of emotion. As already mentioned, the 'I' begins by being fiercely and primarily attached to itself.

This is something of a conundrum, and takes careful thinking through. For example, is it possible to love someone or something without attachment? The common sense answer is, 'No. We are always attached to what and whom we love'. But the correct answer is 'Yes'.

To love something or someone without attachment is a rare form of love. It is the most mature form of love. It is a kind of love utterly free of ambivalence. Completely free of ego, this love is undeniably 'selfless'. It is free of passion, lust, desire, craving and possessiveness. It is fully contented, free beyond any sense of like or dislike, of wanting or not-wanting. It is calm, clear, kind, fresh, certain, innocent, worthy, generous and joyful. It is also attentive, vigilant for the welfare of the beloved. But it is also universal, and therefore seeks to love everything and everybody equally, without preference. This is because, ego-free, it knows no distinction between self and other, between one part of creation and any other. It sees each fragment as interconnected, part of a sacred unity, part of the infinite whole.

This is not to say that mature love, where and when it exists, is without thought and feeling, without judgement and sensitivity. The reverse is true. Love like this embodies compassion and wisdom. It suffers with those who suffer. It understands in ways that take account of every angle, and seems to know intuitively how best to benefit all. It is by no means always passive, but where and when it acts, or refrains from acting, it is in answer to these principles of care and concern. As such, it is never indifferent.

Although secure from the destructiveness of painful emotions, this highly mature form of love is the opposite of unfeeling. It seeks empathically to facilitate conversion of the emotionally painful towards the pain-free, happier side of experience. It is sometimes in a positive sense called 'detached', and this detachment permits it to remain cool and alert, not to turn away but to seek resolution of suffering, conflict and crisis as swiftly, completely and painlessly as possible. But sometimes love like this can only stand helplessly by, and grow wiser. Sometimes, if there seems to be no other way, it will self-lessly give up the life of any among us who feels possessed of this kind of pure love. But anyone truly and knowingly possessed of this kind of love will already have offered up their life to it, considering it a gain to do so rather than any kind of loss. 'To embody this perfect love,' such a person might admit, 'is why I was born'.

The rest of us might envy such a person, especially if we met someone who seemed so imperturbable, so serene and so happy – but, equally, we might not. It seems scary to think that we might at any moment be called upon to die for someone else, especially a stranger, or even to die for a noble cause. How could anyone be happy, we might think, with that possibility hanging over them? Most of us, most of the time, are extremely attached to safety, security and comfort for ourselves, our families and friends. This is natural, but it does leave us open to persistent anxiety and multiple fears.

This rare kind of love is hard to penetrate, hard to understand. It is beyond the reach of the intellect alone, and we get confused when we try to apply it to our own lives. The kind of love we are familiar with tends to be conditional. We even use the word to describe degrees of attachment, saying, for example, 'I like this one, but I really love that one'.

Love in the everyday world is not usually selfless. It is about preferences. It is about attachment and passion. There is no blame or shame in this. It is natural. But it helps us to realise that attachments form the basis of emotional suffering, and that we each have the choice little by little to let go, to develop maturity, to grow wiser, and in the end to be happy. Perhaps we can understand love best in terms of emotion.

The Butterfly of Emotion

24

Experience the time and the place to the full,
Experience everything as it arises and ceases,
Awaken to each moment – and let it go!
This is how to be happy. (B 113)

Here is a butterfly, a symbol of change, hope, maturity. It symbolises spring and summer, playfulness, light, joy and love. This butterfly will help you remember the basic set of rudimentary emotions and the system that links them, dark evolving into light, painful emerging as pain-free, unhappiness maturing, ripening through sorrow into happiness.

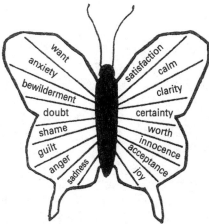

The beating of butterfly wings demonstrates the quicksilver nature of our emotional experience, the potential rapidity of change backwards and forwards in both the nature and strength of the feelings encountered. The blurring of movement indicates a complex merging of simpler emotions into more complicated feelings, thoughts, sense perceptions, actions and words, integrated in some intuitive, mysterious and perfect way.

The stillness of this beautiful creature in repose reminds us to allow our own emotions to settle and find their equilibrium point. It helps us to remember, in such moments of serenity, to seek a point of calm, clarity and joyful contentment, by reaching right down into that inexhaustible well-spring of energy and life that lies both around us and especially within our hearts.

Take a look in any dictionary for words referring directly to human emotion and you will find many. Most are fairly easily reduced to their constituent happy and unhappy origins. Consider, for example, adjectives like puzzled, perplexed, dazed, obtuse, muddle-headed, stumped, flummoxed – hungry, empty, insatiable, intense, keen, eager, earnest, acquisitive, impatient, demanding, bold, impulsive, devoted, fervent, aroused, inflamed, expectant, excited, passionate, infatuated, fanatical, intoxicated, greedy, addicted – timid, uncertain, undecided, sceptical – diffident, embarrassed, shy, bashful, self-conscious, humiliated, mortified – culpable, blameworthy, sinful, remorseful – displeased, fretful, grouchy, prickly, appalled, disgusted, scornful, annoyed, aggressive, contrary, quarrelsome, antagonistic, hostile, loathing, defiant, raging, indignant, cross, irritated, furious, wrathful, exasperated, incensed, fuming, bitter, irate – apprehensive, aghast, agitated, scared, nervous, panicky, alarmed, intimidated, afraid, terrified – subdued, forlorn, upset, hurt, sorry, sore, dejected, embittered, sullen, glum, morose, melancholy, despondent, doleful, woebegone, grim and grave. Cannot all these be filtered through the left wing of the butterfly?

Consider also perceptive, perspicacious, enlightened, far-sighted, meek, moderate, temperate, uncomplaining, receptive, tolerant, grateful, forgiving, restrained, forbearing, dispassionate, imperturbable, cool, steady, composed, placid, unhurried, deliberate, obliging, agreeable, patient, confident, trusting, reliable, genuine, virtuous, moral, impeccable, irreproachable, righteous, chaste, pure, faultless, upright, honourable, proper, innocent, blameless, guileless, tender, affectionate, peaceful, tranquil, non-violent, glad, cheerful, pleased, gratified, gleeful, blithe, sparkling, playful, exhilarated, delighted, ecstatic, enchanted, enthusiastic and sunny. Do these not similarly fit the scheme of the butterfly's right wing?

A Word List of Emotions.

Sit quietly and relax. Take a few minutes to look at the two lists of adjectives. Take first the unhappy ones. Try to separate them according to their constituent rudimentary emotions. Make separate lists if you wish. Some words may fit into more than one of your lists.

Do this again with the happiness list.

Are there words in either case that do not seem to you to fit anywhere? Can you think of any words describing or relating to emotions that are not listed, and that you think cannot be reduced down to having one or more of the eight pairs of emotions at its heart? Make a separate list, either in your mind or on paper.

What, for you, are the constituent emotions of boredom?

Take as little or as much time over this as you wish.

Using the butterfly diagram, whether the balance at rest lies towards happiness or unhappiness, depends on each person's mood and temperament. Moods are relatively temporary, lasting hours or days. They are affected by (and in their turn affect) degrees of fatigue and alertness. Temperament, on the other hand, is a more permanent attribute, the emotional aspect of character or personality.

When we are alone for a while, when there is no one to interact with and no distractions are available, often a particular emotion predominates, happy or unhappy: contentment, joy or tranquillity, say, anger, bewilderment or shame. In everyday life, however, we are more familiar with complex and rapidly changing emotions. The wings of the butterfly seem to be in constant and vigorous motion, different feelings entering the window of our consciousness from moment to moment. In this window we experience changes of energy resulting in sometimes rapid changes in the intensity of feeling from weak to strong or in the reverse direction, from powerful to gentle. Of course there are many different sequences and combinations of the basic emotions, governed by the overall drive of nature towards healing and personal growth.

The point is that any and all possible emotions are made up of combinations of the eight rudimentary pairs as they spontaneously become associated in our minds with thoughts, words, impulses and completed actions. These emotions are driven according to our attachments and aversions, our individual likes and dislikes, which are translated into motivation and meaning, into drives and intentions, into hang-ups and enthusiasms, and into systems of values.

Although such drives and value-systems endure, and form another facet of character or personality, emotions themselves exist only in the moment they are born. They make themselves felt instantaneously, and are communicated equally rapidly to others. They are transmitted empathically, as well as through facial expression and tone of voice, and through specifically emotional behaviours like laughter and crying. These factors obviously play an important part in expanding the effects and range of the eight basic emotions.

Our emotions do not endure without reinforcement, hence their special quality of being both true and immediate. Indeed, complex emotions like boredom and amusement, excitability and composure, impatience and contentment, surprise and serenity have a bearing on how we experience and appreciate the passage of time. Many everyday emotions, including a good number of those listed above, reflect thoughts about the future, anticipation. It is worth repeating that the antidote to confusion is, once again, to keep our minds focused as best we can in the here and now.

Boredom, for instance, seems to involve us in wanting something to happen in the immediate future, coupled with awareness that it is not happening. As well as a form of want, the emotional experience includes an element of frustration – a combination of aversion ('I do not like this.') and mild anger or irritation. There may be doubt and anxiety involved ('Will things ever change for the better?'). We may even feel a little ashamed at being helpless, passive, inert, and unable to make something happen. Boredom, then, may be due to feeling unwanted or unimportant, with the ego being ignored and feeling threatened. It is quite a complex feeling, dependent on both existing and possible future conditions.

Whenever we are not contented, we wish for something exciting to happen to us, or at least to someone with whom we identify ourselves closely. This means something entertaining or arousing which will get our attention, preferably something we like. But this is another form of want, of the desire to be entertained, the desire to be made happy. On close analysis, it is simply another form of suffering, of emotional pain, a form of pain that we ultimately want to escape from.

There is a paradox here. The desire to be made happy by our circumstances; to find and experience pleasure, or simply to gain relief from pain; gets in the way of the natural happiness we already hold and have access to within ourselves. The difference between this genuine happiness and more momentary pleasure we seek in order to evade boredom is that, once we have reached it in ourselves, we see it reflected in, and communicated to, everyone and everything around. Perhaps, while doing some of the exercises in this book, you have already begun to realise this. To realise something is to make it real for yourself. To find happiness within, and access it repeatedly, will not only benefit you but will also inevitably be of benefit to everyone else. In the next chapter we will begin to take a look at the three main ways in which this natural process of finding happiness can become hindered or blocked.

Getting Stuck – Worry, Jealousy, Envy

For happiness' sake,
Pay attention to disturbing and painful emotions,
Be still and watch them settle,
Be still and watch them pass. (B 67)

For most of us, life is a mixture of the routine and the dramatic. How can all the emotions of humour and pathos, comedy and tragedy, fit neatly into an eightfold set of light, happy feelings and their dark, heavy, unhappy counterparts? What of jealousy and envy, for example?

It may help to consider a couple of analogies from art and music. Together with black and white, the colours of the rainbow are all that nature requires. There are no other colours to be found in all the painted masterpieces from every age and culture in the entire world. Include the simple notes of the scale – do, re, mi, fa, so, la, ti, do – and the black notes on the piano, play them in different combinations and sequences, in different rhythms, at varying pitch and volume and what do you have? Each note sounds only for an instant and may last no longer than a few seconds, but each may be repeated over and over, in perhaps an infinite variety of combinations. Potentially all of music is here, and it can of course be played on a very wide range of instruments. Our emotions are something like this, and the different instruments are the many different types of person, the many different kinds of temperament, to be found on our planet.

Temperament is simply the emotional aspect of a person's character or personality, informing and informed by, but distinct from, their thoughts, beliefs and behaviour. Our temperaments differ in terms of balance or settings. In particular, they differ according to whether they are robust and resilient, quick to adjust to change, or slow and more easily upset, perhaps more rigid and fragile. Our temperaments tend to be predominantly either on the happy or unhappy side, with a built-in preference for the lighter or darker colours, the bright or more sombre notes on the scale. Within either the cheerful or solemn sides, there may be a tendency to avoid some notes and prefer others. This is like a piano with some broken or missing notes and others that seem to need hitting harder and more frequently than the rest. Some people seem to be nearly always angry, for example, while avoiding feeling guilty or ashamed.

It is worth remembering that stillness and silence are fundamental both to music and to our emotional lives. Silence and stillness come before either the piano string or the heartstring is set in motion.

Temperamentally Happy or Unhappy?

Sit quietly and reflect on this for a few minutes. It may be easier to think about somebody else, someone you know fairly well. Ask yourself what their natural emotional state is like. Is it light or sombre, happy or unhappy? If unhappy, does one emotion predominate? Can you think of someone, for example, who always seems to be feeling anxious or sad, or any one of the other eight basic emotions? Can you think of any emotions that this person – or you, yourself – seem never or seldom to feel?

Now, can you think of someone who seems perpetually happy? Does this happiness seem to include all of the more pleasant, pain-free emotions?

There is no need to take very long over this. Before you finish the exercise, sit still in silence for a time. Allow your mind to empty of thoughts and distractions. Enjoy the tranquillity for a while.

A person's temperament tends to remain consistent throughout life, but it is not unchangeable. It is best thought of as a starting point from which each of us may mature and ripen. There would be no need for guidance if the natural processes of emotional healing and maturation did not often seem to get blocked. There are three main ways in which such interruption of healing can occur. These involve thoughts, actions and feelings themselves.

Intrusive thoughts, either persistent or recurring, are the basis for what we call 'worry'. Worry is fuelled by anxiety, by the natural emotional response to threat of some kind of loss. When we identify a threat and face up to the loss associated with it, other emotions – doubt, bewilderment, anger and so on – can come into play, leading eventually to sorrow and the start of renewal. Worrying, agonising, being persistently concerned, however, prevents this renewal.

Worry begins with memory and imagination. If you keep your mind focused in the present moment, in the here and now of your breath or your heartbeat, you are much less likely to worry. If anything does threaten us right here and right now, there is no time to worry. We have to act decisively, to get out of the way of a runaway vehicle, for example, or call an engineer if our central heating breaks down in mid-winter.

It is possible to remember vividly a dangerous situation from which we escaped or were rescued, to dwell on it in the imagination and think about what might have happened. At any time we can conjure up worry like this, based on all kinds of potential threats to life, safety, health, kin, possessions, position, image – to whatever we might be attached to. 'Where your treasure is, there will your heart – and thoughts – be also', as it says in the Bible.[10] We must work through worry like this. This means allowing, perhaps encouraging, all the emotions of the cycle, first in the dark phase, then in the light. Often we have to go through this several times before our thoughts settle and become clear. Only when our thoughts are settled and our minds are clear will we be able to discern and follow the correct actions, words and deeds that contribute to harmony, peace and joy. When such discernment is ours, constructive and happiness-promoting behaviour is likely to follow. We are much less likely to make any mistakes.

*

Thinking about keeping what we have and attracting or gathering more also prevents the natural flow of our emotions. These preoccupations inhibit emotional reactivity and block our passage to happiness, however much we may persuade ourselves that we will only be happy when we get what we want.

Consider envy and jealousy for a moment. These are both complex forms of want, of desire, of wishing that things were other than the

---

[10] Matt 6 v 21.

way they happen to be. They are also forms of not-wanting, of aversion, of failure to accept a given situation.

Envy involves wanting what someone else has, perhaps wanting to be like someone else. It begins with a desire for something you do not have – health, youth, beauty, fortune, wealth, success, power, possessions or fame – and the thought that someone else does have whatever it is that you want. Envy can be quite benign, close to admiration and involving respect, but it can also be close to resentment, the basis of which is a feeling of anger. Anger within us towards another often means painful suffering for both.

Jealousy is similar to envy, but it often involves at least three people, hence the potential for even more suffering. Jealousy involves a sense of possession or ownership, usually over a member of the opposite sex. It involves a sense of rivalry.

Jealousy is based on anxiety, on the fear of losing a valued but insecure possession to someone else. This other person, perhaps because they seem more attractive somehow, is often someone we both distrust and envy. Also, because the person of whom we are jealous seems more attractive than we are, doubt and suspicion grow between us and the object of our desire, the person we want to hold onto. Feelings for ourselves may also then degenerate into bitter worthlessness, guilt and shame.

Passion, lust, desire, greed, grasping, covetousness, jealousy, envy, resentment, anger, doubt, mistrust, suspiciousness, shame, worthlessness, guilt, anguish and confusion: all these are inter-connected. They compose the very picture of misery, of depression and despair, within which a sense of hopelessness may also soon be a part.

The antidotes to envy and jealousy are to curb desire, to learn to be satisfied with what we have, and to live as best we can in the present moment. Remember the following phrase from Chapter 14. It could be useful as a motto:

'I want to be free more than I want what I want'.

Why not say the sentence to yourself now, and repeat it as often as you think it might help, whenever you are experiencing some kind of temptation that you think it really better to resist? The truly happy person lives focused entirely in the here and now, untroubled by thoughts of what might be, ignorant of remembered or imaginary threats and losses, free from anxiety, free from fear, free from worry. Regular practice, sitting in stillness and silence, will take each of us step by step nearer this goal.

Worry and Ambivalence – Sandra's Story

Wishing, desire, passion, lust,
Who is not constantly subject to these?
These are what trouble the mind. (H 94)

Unless we take the trouble to keep our minds relatively clear, our thoughts tend to recur, to present themselves again and again for re-thinking. This is the beginning of worry. It is associated with confusion, bewilderment, perplexity. Such thoughts will tend to be influenced by one or more of the other rudimentary emotions, particularly doubt, anxiety and anger. It is often helpful for us to identify the emotions underlying our persistent and troublesome thoughts, then they can more easily and bravely be faced, experienced and exhausted.

When painful emotions are faced in this courageous way, they begin giving up their energy. Sometimes, especially at first, it seems as if they are strengthening, increasing their grip, but this is an illusion brought on by lack of familiarity. You can be reassured that there is no danger of emotional overload. We are protected by the mechanisms of catharsis, of emotional release.

Once a painful emotion begins to lose its energy, the natural process of healing begins again, however locked up it may have been by persistent thoughts. The painful emotions are transformed little by little into their opposites, and a new emotional equilibrium point is set for the future, at least a step or two towards equanimity and resilience, towards the happier side. Painful feelings continue to be felt as painful situations arise. They may now be felt even more keenly, because we are less inhibited about them, knowing they can no longer do us any lasting injury. But their duration is briefer. Because we no longer seek to avoid them, we do not worry about them so much. This is helpful, but there are still two more ways in which our processes of emotional healing and resolution can get blocked.

What Do You Worry About?

Sit quietly or go for a walk on your own. Avoid disturbance and give yourself over for a time to the subject of worry. What do you worry about?

Bring a topic to mind that causes you habitual concern. Look within it for the constituent emotions. Is there anxiety? Try and clarify what this means to you in terms of specific fears. What might happen? What specific threat gives rise to your anxiety? What are the possible losses causing concern? Name the people you are frightened for. (Of course, this includes yourself.)

Now, take a moment to face this anxiety and these fears. Notice any resistance. Notice any doubts, any anger or other feelings that arise.

Stay with the feelings. Be patient with them. Identify them if you can – but more importantly really feel them. Experience them to the full. Do this for as long as it takes the energy in these painful and unwanted feelings to diminish and evaporate. (If this seems to be taking too long, focus on your breath, your heartbeat or your mantra and wait until you feel calm again. You can return to the exercise later.)

Now, delay a little longer in the calm after this mini-squall (or raging tempest) you have brought on yourself. Is your mind any clearer? Have you learned something to your advantage? If not, you may try repeating the exercise. Do calmer and happier thoughts eventually begin to enter your mind? Are you feeling a little more confident? If so, this is a genuine achievement. Don't worry if this does not seem to have worked for you this time. Whether it has or it hasn't, when you are ready, please go back to your life.

'I want to be happy.' This is an emotion about an emotion. Having feelings about feelings is natural and common, but it is also another way for us to impede our natural processes of emotional healing and growth.

Sandra, a woman in her early thirties, wanted very much to be married, but did not feel she had yet met the right man. After leaving college she began working as a photographer, and soon found herself wanting to photograph weddings. At first she enjoyed it, but as time went by she became increasingly ambivalent about her work. She described this to a friend one day. 'I like my job, but also I sometimes hate it. That is because I always end up feeling envious of the bride, and guilty for feeling this envy, and ashamed that I am so envious as to feel guilty about it. It does not seem right that this is what I get paid to do.'

It does not seem right to say no to desire. It is natural to want things. The problem here is one of balance. In Sandra's case the desire to be married has got out of hand. It has become a kind of craving.

The point to note is that this is a preoccupation with something happening (or not happening) in the future. One remedy for Sandra then is to maintain awareness in the present, and not dwell on whatever may enter her imagination. This is difficult for her, because her job necessitates contact with material that fuels her imagination on a regular basis. It is also difficult because she has had no practice at this. She has not yet learned a technique for stilling and focusing her mind. If she had, and had kept a routine of sitting for a while undistracted every day, she would probably have been better placed to deal with her emotional problem. Indeed it may not have arisen.

As well as a powerful and persistent sense of wanting something, some of her basic emotions were stuck in a kind of loop from which she could not escape. Desire translated into envy, envy into shame and shame into guilt, bringing her back to awareness of her intense want (to be married) once again. For her, it was like being in a kind of maze, but one she began to suspect had no way out. She began to experience not only bewilderment and confusion, but also doubt and despair. At the worst moments, she also felt significant levels of anxiety, almost to the point of panic. It helped to have her friend reason with her and calm her down.

The missing emotion was anger. Resolution and healing could not occur because Sandra seldom got angry, either with others or with herself. This was her hidden emotional loop. Other people's anger made her afraid. Whenever anger was directed at her, it made her feel worthless, deeply ashamed. If she ever came close to anger herself, she felt both shame and near-terror. She imagined that if she became angry and showed it, everyone would reject her. She would drive people away, especially potential boyfriends, leaving herself tragically alone and in misery.

This was the hidden fear that was fuelling Sandra's powerful desire to be married. Marriage seemed to her like the only possible solution. With a husband, so her reasoning went, she would never again be alone. But, of course, there were lingering doubts. Marriage, especially to the wrong person, is no guarantee of companionship. Sandra began to realise that she had to become the right person in order to find the right person. She knew she had to mature.

*

As this example shows, anger is a normal and sometimes necessary part of our emotional experience. An aspect of Sandra's temperament was for her to avoid it. In her case this was conditioned by much earlier unpleasant experiences, rather than being an immutable part of her constitution from birth. In other cases there might be an avoidance of shame and guilt, for example, but an excess of anger. The key to enduring happiness is for all painful emotions to be felt in more or less equal measure from time to time, allowing the less sombre, happier and more playful ones to come along in due course.

As Sandra discussed her situation further with her friend, another element also became clear, another aspect of her ambivalence. 'Maybe,' she wondered aloud, 'deep down I don't want to be married.'

Wanting something is always coupled with not-wanting it too, at least in some measure. This is ambivalence. Sandra had begun encountering older women who had never married. Taking an interest in them, she discovered that they were usually both independent-minded and happy. Often they had achieved considerably during their lives, for their own benefit and for the benefit of others. Sandra discovered that she liked, admired and also to some extent envied women like these. 'They are not tied down,' she said to her friend. 'They are all so liberated, so free.'

Initially, sentiments like these added to Sandra's doubts and confusion about herself, and about what she really wanted as her life continued to unfold. Her despair deepened and she found herself sometimes spontaneously depressed to the point of tears. She felt worse, and did not know that this feeling bad was in fact the beginning of her way out.

Unable to control things in her life, to find and hold onto the right man, Sandra remained attached to her hopes and dreams. Later, staving off doubt and despair, she flirted briefly with the alternative plan, to eschew marriage and stay single, but she was unable to convince herself that this would succeed in her case. Now, unable to control her emotions, no longer able to resist her fears, she had at last begun the process of grieving. There was something – attachment to an idea, an image of herself – that she could no longer sustain.

Her hopes and dreams were not irretrievably lost, but Sandra's attachment to them had to weaken in the face of reality. Genuine sorrow and a profound sense of loss was the result. Nevertheless, she was growing up. She began to admit to herself, as well as to her friend, the kind of perfect marriage she had been dreaming of was something of an illusion. It was not going to solve all her emotional problems. Sorrow, grieving over having to accept reality and give up something cherished for so long, however illusory it might have been, was the one thing that really would help. We will see how in more detail in the next chapter.

Virtue, Wisdom and Love

Be calm, kind, generous, loving!
Watch yourself,
As a mother watches over her child! (B 148)

Love conquers ambivalence. It conquers and cures it through the process of lysis, in other words by dissolving attachments. This love is wise, and sees what is best from all sides at once. It is a mature and universal love, not a self-seeking one. Love like this is not in any way self-centred, divisive or possessive. It is constant, generous, joyful and kind, sympathetic to all. It simply does not know how to discriminate. Typified by acceptance and affirmation, it does not know how to criticize or judge.

Sandra's grief and sorrow, to her surprise, unlocked her ability to feel and express anger with diminishing anxiety and fear of making things worse. At first this caused her concern because the anger was so strong and irrational, but within a few weeks it began to subside. Eventually Sandra was able to assert herself and not simply accept disappointments, insults and injuries from others as she had in the past. She was able to do so with less and less anger and aggression. She grew more confident, less self-conscious and much less deeply ashamed. Feeling better about herself, she found she was properly able to ripen, and to love herself in a mature rather than a defensive way.

Sandra grew less preoccupied with results, with how things were going to turn out. She also became less confused about what she wanted and what she did not want. She felt neutral about more subjects than she had before, less ready antagonistically to take two sides at once and do the impossible, to try and make both work out. It no longer seemed to her important to try and please everybody. She was soon able to think more clearly, to see and accept things and other people as they truly were.

Accepting other people as they were, Sandra no longer needed to measure them against her ideals, wishing they were somehow different. Accepting and loving herself, she was increasingly able to accept and love other people. Her family and friends noticed that she had changed. Becoming both happier and more tolerant, she was also becoming more likeable, popular, easier to relax with and fun. It was not long before she had a new boyfriend.

Talking to a Friend.

You will need a friend for this exercise, someone you respect and feel close to, someone you can begin to trust with your thoughts and feelings. Make a plan to meet your friend for a heart-to-heart talk. (You can also do this with a sympathetic group of your friends if you wish.)

If necessary, possibly because you cannot contact and meet a special friend, or because you do not yet have one, sit quietly alone and reflect on that situation. Be honest with yourself about your feelings. When you are ready, imagine yourself with someone else, a warm, friendly parent-figure perhaps, and continue the exercise in your mind.

Your friend and confidant's task is simply to listen (but you may like to offer her or him a turn in due course).

Now, begin by recounting the story of Sandra as best you can remember it. (You can read it if you prefer.) Stop whenever you like and draw comparisons with yourself. Try and explain which emotions you experience frequently and powerfully, and which you seem to avoid. Tell stories from your own life history. See if you can make them make sense to your friend.

Afterwards, spend some time alone thinking through Sandra's story and your own. What have you learned? And what ambivalences operate now in your life? Resolve to be patient with yourself, remembering that you are probably just like everybody else. Be aware and be patient with your emotions and, as you return to your life, avoid the temptation to think of yourself as better or worse off than others. Watch yourself and compare yourself with yourself over time. Be confident. Day by day, month by month, year by year, you will watch yourself grow.

Resolution and healing of the emotional system can be blocked by feelings themselves getting stuck into loops, as in Sandra's repetitions of envy, shame and guilt. There are many such loops that we get into. For example, to feel guilty when you start feeling good is quite common, as is feeling ashamed when you start to feel bad. The former comes from an unhappy awareness of the suffering of others. The latter has more to do with the idea that you are supposed to be happy, and if you are not, you must in some way be at fault.

Obviously, if you feel guilty and ashamed about both feeling good and feeling bad, you have a problem. You are going to be feeling shame and guilt almost all the time. This is where understanding the scheme of basic emotions can be helpful. Unhappy emotions are natural, useful at times and unavoidable. What we call suffering then has to be accepted, including the suffering of others. Only with the freedom from anxiety that acceptance brings can we engage successfully with suffering. Resistance only serves to reinforce it.

The antidote to shame and guilt is to observe them as calmly as possible, observe and experience them until they soften and are transformed. (You may like to repeat Exercise 2a, 'Exploring Some Difficult Feelings'.) Underlying emotions such as anger and sadness may first be revealed. Eventually, through the processes of lysis and catharsis, self-esteem, feelings of virtue and worth will arise in their place.

*

We have seen how healing and growth can be blocked by emotions about emotions, also by emotion-laden thoughts, preoccupations and worry. The third way emotional release and resolution gets blocked is through speech and action. Problems occur when we say and do destructive things. Often this has to do with timing, when words and deeds are either hasty and premature or unduly delayed.

There are four levels of action. The first, over which at the time we may have little control, is impulse. Based on deeply ingrained predilections and values, impulse is immediate, somehow intuitive and often powerful. Change at this level of the system requires a prolonged and consistent influence in one direction or another, or alternatively a sudden and major impact, as in some kind of conversion experience.

The second level of action is that of conscious intention. We think about doing (or not doing) something. We have more control here, and can in particular train our minds in the direction of either selfless and good or selfish and less good (even evil) intention.

The third level is speech. We can put our intentions into words, or refrain from doing so.

The fourth and final level is action (or inaction) itself. In these last two, our degree of control is less general. It can be applied to specific situations and circumstances, right down to the very particular. Our level of choice depends again on our degree of practice and skill. To some extent this defines our degree of maturity.

When we get upset, it takes a while for our thoughts and feelings to settle. Speech and action risk becoming either over-impulsive or paralysed at such times. If we are patient, however, we are less likely to make mistakes, to act or fail to act in ways we might later regret.

This is where prevention is better than cure, where a regular (preferably daily) practice of sitting calmly, still and silent, gives us an advantage. This enables us to retrain ourselves at the very deepest levels of impulse and intention. In doing so we provide ourselves with greater freedom and choice concerning our speech and our actions.

In terms of both thought and emotion, this discipline enables us to develop an increasing capacity for pausing momentarily. This allows us to regain our balance and decide which emotion to follow, to decide what to say and do next. Even when the motor is racing, so to speak, and feelings are running high, we are still able to activate the clutch, to reduce the drive to the wheels, to remain in control.

Speak or act impulsively, without regaining equilibrium, without proper thought or reflection, and we are at the mercy of our emotions. Words and actions based on desire or aversion, doubt or confusion, fear or anxiety, anger, guilt, shame or sorrow will perpetuate suffering. If we wait, however, until we are calm and clear-headed once more, we will feel in control. Neither premature and impulsive, nor unduly withheld or delayed, our words and actions are all the more likely to be both timely and appropriate. We are less likely to say and do what is damaging and destructive. Our words – and our silences – will be sympathetic, healing and kind. Our actions will not be threatening. They will instead be helpful and generous, perhaps first offering and then actually providing support. Everyone benefits as a result.

Emotions are infectious, difficult to ignore, and the situation is even more serious when painful feelings are deeply ingrained. This may be due to temperament or previous unpleasant experiences. Both biological and environmental sets of conditions naturally interact over time. In these cases, impulses, intentions, words and actions are strongly influenced, even dominated by various forms of unhappiness. It is hard for us to avoid this to some degree. Even if it is others who are unhappy, this still affects us. We empathise because we are emotionally sensitive, and on occasions we are likely find ourselves treated inconsiderately by those who are angry or in pain. But there is a way to deal with this so as to remain calm and happy. It is the way of equanimity, of resilience, of allowing our feelings to flow and find resolution.

*

We are so familiar with want, desire and craving that we see it as normal – both within ourselves and in others. It is also sanctioned by materialistic values associated with our modern way of life. As we have discovered, such craving is hard to satisfy. It always seems to recur. Indeed it is possible almost unconsciously to be attracted and attached to addiction itself. Fortunately, there is a way out, a way of escape from this maze of confusion. It is the way of wisdom, the way of happiness.

We are also familiar with not-wanting. If it is entrenched, this aversion breeds deep-seated intolerance, division and hatred. So many people are either conditioned or, perhaps worse, seem to choose to live this way, dividing everything and everyone into what they like and what they dislike, into 'me and mine', 'us' against 'them'. This is a recipe for the continuation of suffering but again, happily, there is an achievable way out.

Words and actions based upon anger and aversion can be both materially and psychologically destructive to oneself as well as to other people, whether we see them as friends or enemies. Causing any harm, especially when we are aware of it, and when we identify even a little with the victims, puts us at risk of feeling some measure of shame and guilt. Once it has happened, the way out of this is through sorrow, through regret, and by apology for actual or threatened harm done. This remedy includes reparation, perhaps offering some kind of compensation as well as by making amends.

It is of course better, wiser and more compassionate to avoid harmful words and actions in the first place. We need to cultivate a vigilant attitude towards our deep-seated impulses and intentions. We need to develop skills to control and reduce what is destructive, and to promote what is healthy and healing. This means eschewing negative words and actions and avoiding both carelessness and indifference.

There are times, for example, when inaction and failure to speak up contribute to suffering. If our silence and passivity serve to collude with wrongdoers, are we not once again open to feelings of guilt and shame?

Virtue brings peace of mind. The reward of virtuous thoughts, words and actions is happiness. Whether you prefer it this way or not, there can be no other. This is simply how it is. This is the true basis of wisdom – to speak and act as if you were the recipient of your own words, actions, thoughts and intentions. Fortunately, we do not have to prepare for every eventuality, because we already have access to a source of wisdom within.

Wisdom arises with compassion from the same well-spring as contentment and happiness, joy and peace. To visit this fountainhead of kindness and equanimity often is to have our most basic impulses and intentions guided spontaneously and progressively by a profound awareness that we are all alike in our suffering. We are interdependent.

Reach wholeheartedly down into this well far enough, draw refreshing sustenance there, and our intentions, thoughts, words, impulses and actions will inescapably, naturally and increasingly be influenced by this sacred knowledge. All indifference, ambivalence and hatred will be transformed, measure by measure, into blissful, calm, clear, profound, mature, universal and all-encompassing love. Sometimes it feels as if our souls already know this. A mature love of this kind is what we all want.

Danny and Elizabeth – a Story of Wisdom and Love

28

'The Key to the Treasure is the Treasure.'
Your mind is the key. Your mind is the treasure.
Seek yourself in the one mind of the cosmos,
And find the unity of the cosmos within yourself.
Honour this mystery.
Find happiness here and now. (H 132 & B 22)

This is a true story. A man, Danny, fell in love with a woman. The woman, Elizabeth, fell in love with the man. It happened quickly, and there was soon a significant degree of trust and affection between them. This led to greater intimacy and sharing of thoughts, words and behaviour.

Elizabeth lived alone and David often visited her. After a time, for the sake of convenience, she had an extra key made for his use. Their relationship flourished. In time Danny proposed, and they were married. After Elizabeth moved in with Danny, she took back the newly redundant key to her former property and had it gold-plated, returning it to Danny as a symbol of their love. Elizabeth wrote a message for him in the card she gave him with the key: 'There will never be any locks or barriers between us'. Quite soon after this, however, she developed a serious illness, a cancer, for which surgical treatment was not completely successful. Three years later the disease had spread, and, calmly and with courage, Elizabeth eventually died.

Danny was stricken with grief. The delay between diagnosis of the tumour and his Lizzy's death had given him some opportunity to prepare himself, but the blow was a bitter one nevertheless. Little by little he began to recover and to remember more of the happy times they had shared. One night, five or six years after she had died, Danny had a peculiar dream. By coincidence a friend was staying with him at the time. This friend, John, was an experienced psychotherapist, and was used to helping people interpret their dreams. As they sat at breakfast, Danny tried to describe his experience during the night.

He recalled walking in the dream down a narrow street after dark. To his right there was a building behind a wall. It seemed like a large private house, but he did not feel particularly interested in it because he was intent on continuing down the road. Several people seemed to be waiting for him there, although he did not know who they were. As he passed by, he was just aware of a single light in the upper window of the darkened house, and it occurred to him that there might be a woman there. He thought perhaps he had a glimpse of her shadow passing quickly across the window, but when he looked up could see nothing.

In the dream, Danny's attention now turned to the downhill curve of the lane and to the people waiting for him, but as he was leaving the house behind he noticed an upended brick on the path beside the wall. On top of the brick was a key. In the dream he thought nothing of it and walked on, but John stopped him and asked about it. 'Keys are often significant in dreams,' he said. 'Can you think about it some more? Could it be somehow connected to the shadowy woman?'

In a flash Danny remembered Elizabeth, and the gold-plated key she had given him. He even went to fetch the still shiny, golden object from its safe place in another room to show his friend. He remembered Elizabeth's message, 'There will never be any locks or barriers between us', and he remembered the innocence, the purity with which he had loved her, the joy and contentment, the mutuality, the total acceptance of each other.

It was a wonderful and powerful feeling, different from anything Danny had known before, even at the height of his love for Elizabeth. All the components of happiness were present and none of the painful emotions, but this time the feelings were not just connected to his wife. Somehow Danny knew that this loving sense of irrevocable inter-connectedness was present between all human beings, including all those who had died and those not yet born.

Danny knew instantly and unequivocally that there are ultimately no barriers between us, except those we erect ourselves. He knew that at the deepest level we are unified and interdependent, and that the nature of unity is love. This was the true meaning of Elizabeth's gift. Much greater than their personal love, it was transformed into a universal and enduring one. This insight was going to change his life for the better. It began with a kind of euphoria that lasted several days.

Danny found out that it makes a difference to know that you are the same as everybody else, especially when the knowledge rests within your heart and your mind at all times. He discovered that when you know that you are constantly somehow interconnected despite separation in time or space, despite apparent differences of age, gender, race, skin colour, conditioning and culture, then every intention, thought, word and action takes on a new and important significance.

In a way you are forced to take account of everything, and to feel a new sense of responsibility for what you think, feel, say and do. You are much more likely to live in the present. You really come to know, in fact, that you are alive. Your life becomes one of abundance.

Danny also discovered that this kind of knowledge seems to be there within each of us if our minds are open and receptive, if we take the time and trouble to reach down far enough to locate and relate to it – in other words, if we take our good-enough bucket and use a strong and long enough rope.

Observing Other People.

Go out into the world and find a place where you can stand or sit relatively undisturbed and watch the people around you. Be still as you watch and listen. Turn your head from side to side only slowly and gently, or perhaps let only your eyes move. Observe. Pay attention. There is no need to try and think.

Stand or sit back and watch people going about their business for as long as you wish. Watch them in different locations and at different times.

Later, when you are alone again, perhaps at home, sit quietly and reflect on what you have in common with other people like those you have been watching and listening to. Concentrate on the attributes you share. Try and ignore for the moment the ways in which you are different, the things that seem to separate you. Think about the human body, the senses, thoughts, words, ideas, motives, ambitions, actions and, especially, the emotions. How much alike are we in respect of all these? How alike are we all in our ability to experience different emotions?

If you have been able to recognise many similarities with people who at first seem unlike you, how does this make you feel?

Spend as long or as little time as you wish over this. Discuss your thoughts with one or more friends if you like.

During those first few days Danny recognised that, through his dream, Elizabeth's key had revealed a sacred kind of knowledge. He found himself connected in some mysterious way not only to people but also to nature, to all creatures and all of creation. The sensations he felt were of wonder and gratitude as well as joy. Aware of some great universal power, he found himself wanting someone to thank and to praise. He felt love everywhere, and his own capacity for selfless love had increased. He found that others reflected the love back to him. People responded intuitively to Danny's good, happy feelings.

Most of us must take on trust that there is a sacred unity operating in our lives while we continue to seek it out, but Danny met within himself a profound and constant awareness of it. It was with him years later, and had, if anything, grown. This sense of unity, once encountered, forms a secure foundation for the spontaneous development of kindness and generosity. It is natural that compassion and selflessness of thought, word and behaviour arise out of it. The scriptures from all religious traditions say much the same. All great teachers, past and present, all wise people, the saints and the prophets, have tried not only to teach these things but also to embody them in their lives.

Danny's realisation experience was like going through a kind of conversion. The euphoria of the first few days did not wear off, but started to alter gradually and subtly. His joy became tempered with a kind of awe and respect for people and nature, and a powerful sense of gratitude for the gifts of life and the consciousness with which to take it all in. He felt grateful to his parents for bringing him into the world and bringing him up. He felt grateful to Elizabeth for her gifts of sharing and love. He felt grateful to everyone who had helped him along his way in life, and to everyone and everything in a mysterious way just simply for being.

Just as there was no barrier to his love, he could find no barrier to the immensity of his gratitude. And with gratitude came benevolence, the wish for everyone to be well and happy, the intention and desire to live as best he could for the benefit of others, to serve them in little things as in big ones. He grew increasingly considerate towards his local environment and ultimately, the more he thought about it, for everything animate and inanimate throughout the universe.

*

An important quality of Danny's joyful awareness was that of immediacy. He took notice of what was happening both in the world and simultaneously within his own mind in the here and now, in the present moment. He found that he wanted others to share in this joyful and mindful awareness. However, he became increasingly and painfully conscious that so many people were not doing so. Eventually, he began to grow irritated, even angry, at this.

This new recognition of others' pain and suffering was something of a turning point for Danny. Intuitively, empathically, compassionately, he began experiencing unpleasant feelings again in himself. This time, however, he did not attempt so much to resist. He could see the justice, the necessity for his feelings, including anger, so he was able to accommodate them more easily and let them flow through him to find resolution.

Danny also reasoned that you have to know how someone else feels before you can help them. This is the distinction between sympathy, which is how you think you would feel in another person's situation, and empathy, which is a direct, almost telepathic sharing of how another feels at the moment they are feeling it.

Less preoccupied with his own inner world, Danny could now see how people often became and remained preoccupied with what had happened in their past, what was (or might be) happening elsewhere in the present, and with what might happen in the future. He knew that this diversion of the mind away from the here and now was causing them to suffer, whatever the contents of their preoccupations, even if they were on the face of it pleasurable. These people, he knew, were missing out and, instead of feeling smug or self-satisfied, he felt a little sad and confused. He found himself growing increasingly angry and paused to consider the situation. Then he realised that his first priority was to look after himself. Only when his happiness and peace of mind were secure would he be fit to help others.

Without this kind of wisdom trying to do good for others and teach them leads to failure, anger, bitterness, burnout and exhaustion. On the other hand, wisdom without compassion is false. Intelligence, cleverness, wit are not enough, and are often self-seeking. Wisdom cares and, until its ways are properly and thoroughly learned, sometimes it can really hurt. The way to deal with this is simply to keep moving forward, to grow in maturity and wisdom, often by asking for help.

Love, Meaning and Purpose

29

As a raindrop is to the ocean, so people are linked –
Each one to the remainder.
We are the same but different, different but the same.
Each is part of the whole. (B 141,142)

Falling in love is exciting, and feels permanent. 'I will love you forever.' This feels like a genuine sentiment, but it is often perhaps more truthful to say: 'At this moment I *feel* as if I will love you forever'.

Love embodies all the emotional components of happiness – peace of mind, joy and contentment in particular. The mind in love is full of love, taking little or no account of the passage of time. However, unless the love of one person for another is used as a model or template for loving other people – children, family, friends, acquaintances, strangers, and eventually enemies too – it can be called immature, and it is likely one day to falter. If you love someone the best advice is to use that love to find love in your heart for everyone else.

When people first fall in love, desire is usually strong and breeds the wish and intention both to possess and hold onto the other. Anxiety about losing them, or losing their affection, quickly follows. In this situation the love is already impure, self-seeking, jealous and controlling. To develop maturity in love is the task of all who want to find happiness, and of course this involves not just one other person but many.

*

A similar argument holds for values and ideas. It is natural for us to be attracted by ideologies as young adults, to find within ourselves a love for this or that political or religious philosophy, to develop a strong attachment to it, strong convictions about it. But again, good advice is to use this single affection to develop a curiosity about other sets of ideas and to keep our minds as open as possible. This makes for greater tolerance, fewer divisions, peace and much happiness in the world.

This is a way for each of us to count everyone as a friend, perhaps as a teacher of new ideas and not as a rival or an enemy. It is a way of love, a way of peace. Friendship is one of the key ingredients of happiness, and happiness is one of the key ingredients of friendship. Happy people are popular, and so find making friends easy.

Being tolerant and being kind are important. As we tend to like those who we seem to *be* like, we tend also to be kind to those we perceive as similar to us. This is why happiness depends on seeking out similarities between ourselves and others and not focusing so much on distinctions. Although each of us is unique in background, personal history and temperament, at the deepest level – in our souls, as we might say – we are the same.

May I Be Well – and May Others Be Well.

Go and sit alone quietly somewhere. This exercise is in two parts, and the first part can be done in either of two ways, depending on your mood.

If you are feeling at all low or subdued, less than completely happy, begin by sitting upright in a good posture with your eyes almost closed, watching your breath. Imagine the unpleasant feeling to be like a cloud of black smoke gathering in your lungs. Imagine that, with each out-breath, you discharge the contents of your lungs out of your body into the air around you to be quickly dissipated. Now, with each in-breath, imagine taking in an equivalent amount of cool, clear life-giving air, making you feel well and displacing more of the upsetting blackness from your system, ready to be exhaled next time. Continue for at least ten breaths, and no more than about forty. Repeat this later if you wish.

If you are feeling fine at the start (or after the first part of the exercise has been successful), sit upright in a good posture with your eyes almost closed, watching your breath. Imagine the pain and unhappiness of others out there in the world – those known to you and those not, some perhaps far away. Imagine this sorrow and distress as a dark black cloud coming towards you and surrounding you. Your own breath is pure, clean and cool. Imagine on the in-breath taking a lungful of the smoky dark cloud that is neutralised and dissipated within the cleanliness of your body and emotional system. Imagine then on the out-breath that you are exhaling only pure, clean air back out into the world to purify the landscape for others. Continue this for at least ten breaths, and no more than about forty. You may also repeat this later if you wish.

Now, when you are ready for the next part of the exercise, maintain your posture and continue to breathe, and to pay attention to each breath. On each in-breath, say (or whisper silently) to yourself, 'May I be well'. On each out breath say, 'May others be well'. Continue this for between five and twenty minutes.

When performing this exercise, especially after practice, you may find it helpful to bring to mind people you love as you recite softly, 'May others be well'. When this is established, you may then choose to bring to mind people of whom you are less consciously fond, people who are just acquaintances or strangers, for example. Later still, you may be ready to try bringing into mind people you dislike, including people you hate and think of as enemies, continuing to wish others well. When you can do this with equanimity, you will be well on the path towards lasting happiness and contentment.

What gives us a sense of meaning and purpose in our lives? There is probably no satisfactory collective answer to this important question. We have choices, and must discover the options and decide for ourselves. Others can only share experiences and offer advice. Perhaps this observation itself gives us a clue.

A real sense of meaning and purpose in life is essential for psychological health, and does seem to come very largely from a sense of belonging, being a small but significant part of a bigger picture in some way. We seem naturally to want to belong and also to contribute.

Each of us belongs to a family and some kind of social group. We are motivated towards establishing, maintaining and furthering social bonds of one kind or another at home, at work and at leisure. We have choices about how narrowly or broadly we identify with other people, groups and organisations. The more widely we associate, the greater the opportunity to share with, to give and receive from others. What do we share? At the empathic level, it is the full spectrum of the emotions that we share, moving away from pain towards peace, joy and contentment. In the most profound sense, then, what we share with, give to and receive from each other is love. The more mature it is, the better. How does this tie in, if at all, with spirituality?

*

There are powerful arguments to suggest that psychology and spirituality are linked. Both can be described as dimensions of human experience, each of which is at times subordinate to the other. Psychologists are beginning to emphasise that we all have a spiritual nature, in the same way that we have a sexual nature. It is something profoundly fundamental and affecting.

A significant problem in trying to research spirituality, however, is its subjectivity. Spiritual experiences tend to be very personal, somehow fitting exactly and appropriately into the life history of the person concerned, often transforming it in unforeseen ways. As in Danny's case, for example, experiences like these are usually private. Other people, however close at hand, do not share in them directly. They are rare, and hard either to predict or observe in anything like laboratory conditions, so this makes studying them difficult. They are also invisible occurrences beyond ordinary powers of description. Because spirituality is hard to research, though, does not mean that it should be ignored. The 'Butterfly Theory' at the heart of this book (see Chapter 25), may be helpful at this juncture, for example, to link mind and spirit in a plausible way.

The emotions provide an excellent bridge between psychology and spirituality. Such links operate within each mind, and also between all the people of the world community. Our emotions provide the most immediate and incontrovertible connections between our surface distinctions and deep similarities, superficial differences and innermost uniformity. The basic double-set of eight emotions can provide consistency in terms of both intra-personal (individual) and inter-personal (social) psychology.

This consistency of emotion is most apparent when the ego-self drops away. This facilitates the joining of mind and soul to each other and to creation by means of compassion, wisdom and love. To be even faintly aware of this is to discover true meaning and purpose in life. Set yourself on the road to finding the wellspring of happiness within and then around you, and you will know what this means. *The key to the treasure is the treasure.*' As we shall see in the final chapter, this key, this treasure, this wellspring has many names and many routes of approach. As they draw near to the source these paths seem increasingly similar.

Psychology, Spirituality and Religion

Live each moment one at a time,
Guided by sacred knowledge,
By wisdom. (B 73)

Whatever it is that gives a sense of meaning and purpose to the life of each one of us will underpin at the deepest level our daily values, our individual thoughts, impulses, intentions, speech and actions. However we may conceive of this fundamental originating power and ultimate goal – a Key, a Treasure or a Wellspring – it has been called many things. Throughout our history and all over the planet this ultimate source of human happiness, this sacred unifying principle, has had a name.

In Taoism it is called 'The Tao', 'The Way', or, even more enigmatically, 'The Nameless'. In Buddhism it is known as 'Emptiness' or simply 'Mind'. For Native Americans, 'Wakan-Tanka', which might translate as 'Great Spirit' or 'Great Mystery'. The Aramaic word 'Abwoon' (or 'Abwun') means something like 'Sacred Unity', but also 'Cosmic Parent', invoking a personal or personified Divinity.[11]

---

[11] Aramaic has similarities with Hebrew and other middle-eastern languages. It is the language spoken by Jesus. 'Abwoon' is the first word of The Lord's Prayer. (Matt 6 v 9).

Although truly beyond concept, beyond conventional description, the Supreme Being, the Almighty, the Creator, the Godhead, the 'God beyond God' is also called, 'I am', 'Yahweh' and, 'Jehovah' in the Old Testament, 'Allah' by Muslims and Sufis, 'Brahman' by Hindus, 'The Father', 'Christ' ('The Son') and the 'Holy Spirit' – together 'The Holy Trinity' – in the New Testament.

There are many more names for the highest Deity, the One God. According to some religious scholars there are 300 names for God in the Torah, 300 names in the Psalms of David, 300 in the New Testament and 99 in the Qur'an. They are mainly descriptive terms such as 'The All-Seeing', 'The Just', 'The Truth', 'The Eternal' and 'The Loving'. The angels and the prophets are also between them said to know 2000 more secret names.

This is the source of life and love which humankind has revered and worshipped, to which our brothers and sisters have given and continue to give thanks as well as praise. This is the one who has been the focus not only of all our praise and gratitude, both collective and personal, but also of entreaty and prayerful requests for intercession, for advice, for healing, help, strength and support.

When we call upon this God, named or nameless, in silence and stillness, what we do may be thought of as meditation or prayer. There is in almost every religion a considerable meditative tradition. In silence we begin to feel calm, serenity, contentment, clarity of mind, wonder, reverence, respect, innocence, esteem for self and others, loving-kindness, faith, joy, gratitude and freedom. We are naturally being healed not only emotionally but also physically, mentally and spiritually. To be free from want is to be free indeed. To be free from doubt and bewilderment, passion, desire and aversion, anxiety, anger and hatred, shame, guilt and sorrow is not only to be deeply happy, it is also to enjoy magnificent psychological health.

Many of us either independently or together, are seeking health and freedom. Where people come together successfully as a group in this search there will be fellowship, friendship and a welcome for others, a natural wish to share the benefits. Organisations like this which attract sympathetic or like-minded people can act as networks of support, and can be treasure-houses of knowledge and wisdom. In choosing to live and work together, the people involved provide each other with fellowship and community. Worshipping together, perhaps reading scripture together, offering praise and thanks for all that seems sacred and holy, asking for help and forgiveness; this all seems natural to those involved. It is how churches and religions develop. But problems can arise when there is exclusivity, when people are turned away or when new ideas are rejected. This is when the walls of the well begin to crumble, the bucket grows rusty and leaks, the rope becomes frayed and rotting, too short and weak to reach the life-giving stream. Organisations based on a philosophical, political or religious ideology can become intolerant and possessive, exclusive and defensive, belligerent and oppressive. On the other hand, if their members stay in touch with the true origin of universal wisdom and love, however it is conceived – as an inexhaustible wellspring or as a supreme being – such an organisation is likely to be of incomparable benefit to all.

Many people start to feel within themselves a sense of mission or service, perhaps to assist the sick and needy, to teach, to preserve the environment, to eschew discrimination, to embody goodwill to all and, above all, to be happy.

If they are wise and truly selfless, such people will say to others, 'This is what helps me. Why not try it for yourself? We will help you understand these ideas and put them into practice if you want. Otherwise what we want is only for you to be free.' There will be no need to dominate or insist. Others will be attracted by their openness, wisdom, kindly compassion and joy. This is the test of a true religion and of a true teacher. It works. There is no need for anyone to be pushy.

Most people are born into or raised within a comprehensive ideological tradition, perhaps one of the main world religions – Hinduism, Buddhism, Judaism, Christianity and Islam. Each of these contains different sects or denominations, and most have given rise to newer versions.[12] The potential for confusion and bewilderment is considerable. It seems best for each of us to begin by looking into whatever is most available and familiar, especially if there are good teachers at hand, even if it may seem irrelevant or boring, even partially (perhaps completely) wrong. As well as learning from what is right, we can also learn from what seems to be wrong by carefully discerning the flaws as we see them.

Whatever religion or humanitarian faith you are exposed to, in childhood or later, whether it seems to be for you or not, offers someone a path through it to the heartland, to the wellspring of joy and enlightenment. We do well to remember this, and to try and respect all faiths and religions. If your own tradition does not seem

---

[12] For example, Guru Nanak (b 1469) founded Sikhism in India as an attempt to unite Hindus and Muslims. Baha'ism, dating from 1844, has the aim of uniting all world religions. In 1830, Joseph Smith founded the Church of Jesus Christ of Latter-day Saints in North America with marked differences from, and additions to, conventional Christianity.

satisfactory, you might seek out, or wait patiently for an encounter with a teacher or group that feels more appropriate. It is sensible not to make a commitment too quickly, however, for sadly there are many false teachers, prophets and leaders at large in the world. Good advice is to look for a group with an extensive and successful tradition, whose members seem to be happy.

Renewal of Meaning and Purpose – Reflections on Religion and Spirituality.

Sit quietly. When you are calm and undistracted, turn your thoughts to your own upbringing and tradition. Was there a religious or spiritual component? How did you respond to it then? How do you feel about it now?

Would you say you are knowledgeable about your religious or spiritual background? Have you explored it fully? Are you familiar with its scriptures? Have you read any recently? Have you kept up any kind of spiritual practice? Have you explored any other religious tradition or practice?

Take your time thinking these matters through. They are relevant to the search for happiness. It is common for people to grow dismissive of their own religion for a variety of reasons. If this is the case, be honest with yourself about it. Even if you are still practising your faith, ask yourself how fresh and alive it seems, or how much it may have become just a routine.

Now think again about the founders of your religion and their intentions. Reflect deeply on the original teachings. Ask yourself truthfully how much your faith or religious tradition has in common at this basic and essential level with other traditions, those that you know about as well as those you do not yet know about. You may need to read other scriptures and visit the holy places of other religions with an open mind. Of course, you may first wish to visit, or revisit, some of the scripture and pilgrimage sites of your own.

If this does not appeal, if you constantly desire to be entertained, if you want sense pleasures, material objects, wealth, fame and success more than peace, and joyful freedom from want and desire, more than freedom from the burdens of aversion as well as those of attachment, ask yourself calmly now how and why this may be. Maintain equanimity. Return to the breath and the present moment if you need to. Try not to let your ego-self trick you. (Ask yourself, for example, what will possessions and success matter an hour, a day or a decade after your eventual death.)

If you find yourself confused in the face of religion and spirituality, or afraid, insecure, doubtful, even angry, take a few moments to reflect on how these are just feelings, emotions which may well be transformed into their pain-free complementary forms in the course of your search. Ask yourself what you might have to gain, especially in terms of a renewed and replenished sense of belonging, of meaning and purpose, from discovering a sacred unity of wisdom, compassion and love in everyone's heart and mind as well as your own? Take as long over all this as you wish.

Many spiritual institutions recommend a set of rules, 'precepts' or guidelines for behaviour. The simplest amount to the following:

1 Be mindful at all times – watch closely your intentions, thoughts, words and actions.
2 Avoid harmful speech – swearing, gossiping and telling lies (including not telling the truth).
3 Avoid doing harm. Always seek opportunities to help and do good. In particular avoid aggression – even more important, avoid taking life.
4 Control your desire for what is not yours. Avoid taking what has not been offered or given.
5 Avoid sexual misconduct. There is great potential, which is not easily seen and accepted at the time, perhaps in the heat of passion, for bringing harm, emotional pain, shame and guilt upon yourself and others, hence this advice.
6 Avoid intoxicating substances. They induce craving and reduce your capacity for vigilance, for maintaining selfless intentions and for restraining excessive, shameful, dissolute or otherwise harmful behaviour or language. Also, in seeming to offer a substitute for genuine happiness, they may divert people away from the right track.[13]

If we are still inexperienced and immature, we might be tempted to think that these recommendations spoil our fun, but many have discovered that the consequence of ignoring them is not lasting happiness but misery. Good relationships depend on being honest and

[13] Only with great discipline, skill and maturity – or under appropriate guidance – can a person use alcohol or drugs safely in the proper service of spirituality.

considerate towards one another. Every successful society has had (or still has) these basic rules at its heart. They are the necessary principles and values for survival and a successful social existence, as well as the foundation that underpins happiness. They are values not only for today but for all time. They are not commandments to be thought of as absolute and compulsory. They are simply tried and trusted recommendations that arise out of wisdom.

*

Finally to further your quest for happiness, make a point of observing nature. Find and cultivate within yourself a relationship with the natural world, with the sun, moon and stars, hills, mountains, rivers, valleys, plains and oceans, with the bounty of plant and animal life that depends on these things and on which we depend in our turn. Reflect on this saying from Buddhism – 'All that arises ceases'. Watch. Observe the truth of it. Be still and silent from time to time. Reflect upon all of these wonders.

Make a point of observing others, strangers as well as those close to you. Watch people with the aim of recognising similarities more and more, so that you can spontaneously offer a natural and true friendship to others because you know that you are alike. We are alike in a deep and fundamental way in our emotions, in our minds, in our hearts, in our soul.

Remember that we are all the same but different, different but the same. The remedy for mixed feelings – for any kind of ambivalence, towards ourselves, each other, towards nature, the universe, or towards a named or nameless God – is love. This cure is ripe, mature love, selfless love, a virtuous love free of doubt, embodying calm, happiness and contentment.

No-one is alone, but each person has a unique personal history and suffers the inclinations of an individual temperament. You are wise therefore to reflect on and adapt for yourself the suggestions and ideas in this book, which is intended as a guide offering direction, hope and encouragement. Read again the chapters and repeat the exercises you may find useful. Why not grant yourself the freedom that comes from applying a little discipline? Individual effort is required to find and reach the wellspring of happiness, but you have already begun. Teach yourself not to hinder your emotions but to facilitate and observe them, to encourage, to *suffer* them in every way. Watch with increasing equanimity. Feel them gradually resolve as you gain, step by step, in emotional maturity and resilience. Experience new levels of contentment.

'You only get out of life what you put into it', as my father's dictum has it. Step out now. Take your bearings and put a foot bravely forward. Go *'Reap what you sow'*. Reap for your own benefit, for the benefit of others, for the benefit of all. Reap joy, confidence and peace, equanimity, clarity of mind and an inviolable sense of personal worth. Work your way to happiness gradually, by being awake and aware, by practising stillness and silence – and by living your life.

The key to the treasure is the treasure. Your mind is the key. Your mind holds the treasure. This is the way.

Finally, think again about this. Every ending is a new beginning. And remember, you have to start where you are.

Resources

MENTAL HEALTH ADVICE

If you experience painful emotions which are severe or persist, please ask someone for help and advice. There is plenty available.

First, try local health centre, **your family doctor** or NHS Direct, particularly if your pattern of sleep or your appetite is upset, also if you have any physical symptoms such as dizziness, breathing difficulty, atypical pain or bowel disturbances.

Professional counsellors usually advertise in Yellow Pages and other local directories. It is important to find one you like and feel confident with.

Alternative or complementary therapies, such as aromatherapy and massage, acupuncture and so on can be helpful. Look for advertisements in telephone directories, the local press and health food shops.

Do not forget the value of **exercise.** Visit your local swimming pool, health centre or gym. This is part of normal mental health hygiene. It involves working at keeping your mind in good shape as well as your body.

Other resources may be found through your local Citizen's Advice Bureau, library or mental health telephone helpline.

National organisations providing advice, training, leaflets or factsheets include:

MIND, Granta House, 15–19, Broadway, London, E15 4BQ.
Tel: 0208 519 2122. See website: *www.mind.org.uk/information*

The Samaritans, 10, The Grove, Slough, Berks, SL1 1QP.
Tel: 01753 532713.

CRUSE – Bereavement Care, 126, Sheen Road, Richmond, Surrey, TW9 1UR. Tel: 0208 940 4818.

Young Minds, 102–108, Clerkenwell Road, London, EC1M 5SA.
Tel: 0207 336 8445. Helpline: 0800 018 2138. For parents concerned about the mental and emotional health of their children.

Compassionate Friends, 53, North Street, Bristol, BS3 1EN.
Tel: 01179 539639. For bereaved parents who have lost a child.

SANE, 2nd Floor, 199–205, Old Marylebone Road, London, NW7 5QD.
Tel: 0207 724 6520. Saneline (London) 0207 724 8000. Saneline (elsewhere) 0845 767 8000.

The Royal College of Psychiatrists, 17, Belgrave Square, London, SW1X 8PG. Tel: 0207 235 2351. See website: *www.rcpsych.ac.uk/info*

BOOKS

Bhagavad Gita: The Song of God, trans. Isherwood, C and Prabhavananda, Swami, fourth edn., Vedanta Press, Hollywood, California, 1987.

Bible Societies, The, *New Life: The Good News Bible*, Collins/Fontana, 1976

Dalai Lama, The, His Holiness, and Cutler, H, *The Art of Happiness*, Riverhead, 1999.

de Mello, A, *Sadhana: A Way to God, Christian Exercises in Eastern Form*, Image Books, New York, 1984.

Dhammapada, The: The Sayings of the Buddha, trans. Byrom, T, Vintage, New York, 1976.

Douglas-Klotz, N, *The Hidden Gospel: Decoding the Spiritual Message of the Aramaic Jesus*, Quest, Wheaton, Illinois, 1999.

Hanh, Thich Nhat, *Present Moment, Wonderful Moment*, Rider, London, 1993.

Hanh, Thich Nhat, *Peace is Every Step: The Path of Mindfulness in Everyday Life*, Rider, London, 1991.

Holden, R, *Happiness Now!*, Hodder & Stoughton, London, 1998

I Ching, The, trans. Wilhelm, R and Baynes, C, third edn., Princeton University Press, Princeton, New Jersey, 1967.

Linn, D, *Altars: Bringing Sacred Shrines Into Your Everyday Life*, Rider, London, 1999.

Rinpoche, Sogyal, *The Tibetan Book of Living and Dying*, Rider, London, 1992.

Scott-Peck, M, *The Road Less Travelled: The New Psychology of Love, Traditional Values and Spiritual Growth*, Rider, London, 1990.

Teresa, Mother, *A Simple Path*, Ballantine, New York, 1995.

Tsu, Chuang, *Inner Chapters*, trans. Feng, G and English, J, Wildwood House, London, 1974.

West, E. *Happiness Here and Now: The Eightfold Path of Jesus Revisited With Buddhist Insights*, Continuum, New York and London, 2000.

Whiteacre, S, *The Good Retreat Guide*, Rider, London, 2000.

Whiteside, P, *The Little Book of Happiness*, Rider, London, 1998.

——*The Little Book of Bliss*, Rider, London, 2000.

Zohar, D and Marshall, I, *SQ – Spiritual Intelligence*, Bloomsbury, London, 2000

GROUPS AND ORGANISATIONS

Christian meditation:

The Julian Meetings, c/o G Ballinger, The Rectory, Kingstone, Hereford, HR2 9EY. UK-wide network of meditation groups. See website: *www. julianmeetings.org*

The World Community for Christian Meditation (WCCM), UK Office, 23, Kensington Square, London, W8 5HN. Tel/fax 0207 376 1637. Also has a network of meditation groups, based on the teachings of Benedictine Father John Main. See website: *www.wccm.org*

Buddhist meditation:

Sharpham College, Ashprington, Totnes, Devon, TQ9 7UT. Tel/fax 01803 732037. Residential courses.

The Buddhist Society, 58 Eccleston Square, London, SW1V 1PH. Tel 0207 834 5858. Publishes *The Middle Way* journal. See website: *www.buddsoc.org*

Rigpa, 330 Caledonian Road, London, N1 1BB. Tel 0207 700 0185. Tibetan Buddhism.

Tibet Foundation, 10 Bloomsbury Way, London, WC1A 2SH. Tel 0207 404 2889. For information on Tibetan Buddhism and culture. See website: *www.tibet-foundation.org*

Amaravati Monastery, Great Gaddesden, Hemel Hempstead, Herts, HP1 3BZ. Tel 01442 84255 (office), 843411 (guest info), 843239 (retreat info). Theravada Buddhist tradition – mainly Western monks and nuns, 'The Forest Sangha'. Links with other monasteries offering teaching, meditation and retreats throughout UK and worldwide. See websites: *www.FSnews.cjb.net* and *www.ratanigiri.org*

Meditation and teaching from other traditions:

The School of Meditation, 158 Holland Park Avenue, London, W11 4UH. Tel 020 7603 6116. See website: *www.schoolofmeditation.org*

LIFE Foundation School of Therapeutics, Maristowe House, Dover Street, Bilston, West Midlands, WV14 6AL. Tel 01902 409164. Founded by Dr Mansukh Patel and associates in 1978 to promote meditation, yoga and holistic health care. Excellent annual conference in July.

Abwoon Study Circle, c/o The Green House, 45 The Roman Way, Glastonbury, BA6 8AB. Fosters peace through the wisdom of the Middle Eastern traditions. See website: *www.abwoon.com*

Brahma Kumaris World Spiritual University, Global Co-operation House, 65 Pound Lane, London, NW10 2HH. Tel 0208 727 3350. An international organisation offering meditation training, retreats and much more. See website: *www.bkwsu.com*

Other organisations of interest:

Buddhist-Christian Network, Delfryd, Llanbedrog, Pwllheli, Gwgnedd, North Wales, LL53 7UA. Tel 01758 740694. email *ewest@onetal.net.uk* Regular newsletter, information and meetings.

The Thomas Merton Society of Great Britain and Ireland, c/o The Membership Secretary, TMS, Flat 13, The Old Courtyard, St Nicholas Hospital, Salisbury, Wiltshire, SP1 2SW. Publishes *The Merton Journal*. Holds local, national and international meetings, linked with the worldwide Thomas Merton Society. See websites: *www.stop.at/thomasmerton*, *www.merton.org* and *www.mertonfoundation.org*

The Scientific and Medical Network, c/o The Administrative Director, Lake House, Oakley, Near Dorking, Surrey, RH5 5NS. Aims to deepen understanding in science, medicine and education through both rational analysis and intuitive insights. Links like-minded individuals, encouraging the exchange of ideas and the cultivation of friendship. Publishes *Network*, and holds local, national and international conferences. See website: *www.scimednet.org*

TRAVEL

Soul of India Tours Ltd, Freepost MID 17830, Wolverhampton, WV1 7BR. Tel/Fax 01902 561485. email *info@soulofindia.com*. Website: *www.soulof india.com* 'Sacred sites and spiritual discovery for independent travellers.'

ADDITIONAL WEBSITES

Learn about mental health and mental illness at both:
  www.mentalhealth.com and
  http://easyweb.easynet.co.uk/simplesych

www.ementalhealth.com
www.nsf.org.uk/conditions
www.nimh.nih.gov/public/index.cfm

The Scientific and Medical Network is at:
www.scimednet.org

Find out about Christian meditation at:
www.retreats.org.uk

Investigate Buddhism at:
www.buddhanet.net
www.BuddhaMind.cjb.net
www.tricycle.com

Discover Thich Nhat Hanh and the UK Community of Interbeing at:
www.interbeing.org.uk

Robert Holden (author of *Happiness Now!*) at:
www.happiness.co.uk

Updated website details and additional resources:
www.happinesssite.com